6.90

D1294482

TROILUS AND CRESSIDA
OR, TRUTH FOUND TOO LATE

BY JOHN DRYDEN

1679

A FACSIMILE PUBLISHED BY CORNMARKET PRESS
FROM THE COPY IN THE BIRMINGHAM SHAKESPEARE LIBRARY
LONDON
1969

PUBLISHED BY CORNMARKET PRESS LIMITED
42/43 CONDUIT STREET LONDON W1R ONL
PRINTED IN ENGLAND BY FLETCHER & SON LTD, NORWICH

SBN 7191 0189 1

TROILUS

AND

CRESSIDA,

OR,

TRUTH Found too Late.

A

TRAGEDY

As it is Acted at the

Dukes Theatre.

To which is Prefix'd, A Preface Containing
the Grounds of Criticism in Tragedy.

Written By *JOHN DRYDEN*
Servant to his Majesty.

---

*Rectius, Iliacum carmen deducis in actus,
Quam si proferres ignota indictaque primus*, Hor.

London, Printed for *Abel Swall* at the Unicorn at the West-
end of S. *Pauls*. and *Jacob Tonson* at the *Judges Head* in *Chan-
cery lane* near *Fleet-street*, 1679.

TO THE
RIGHT HONOURABLE
ROBERT
EARL OF
Sunderland,

Principall Secretary of State, One of His Majesties most Honourable Privy Council, &c.

My Lord,

SInce I cannot promise you much of Poetry in my Play, 'tis but reasonable that I shou'd secure you from any part of it in my Dedication. And indeed I cannot better distinguish the exactness of your taste from that of other men, than by the plainness and sincerity of my Address. I must keep my Hyperboles in reserve for men of other understandings : An hungry Appetite after praise : and a strong digestion of it, will bear the grossnesse of that diet : But one of so criticall a judgement as your Lordship, who can set the bounds of just and proper in every subject, would give me small encouragement for so bold an undertaking. I more than suspect, my Lord, that you wou'd not do common Justice to your self : and therefore, were I to give that Character of you, which I think you truly merit, I wou'd make my appeal from your Lordship to the Reader, and wou'd justify my self from flattery by the publique voice, whatever protestation you might enter to the contrary But I find am to take other measures with your Lordship ; I am to stand upon my guard with you, and to approach you as warily as *Horace* did *Augustus.*

Cui

The Epiſtle Dedicatory.

Qui male ſi palpere, recalcitrat undique tutus.

An ill tim'd, or an extravagant commendation, wou'd not paſs upon you: but you wou'd keep off ſuch a Dedicator at arms end; and ſend him back with his *Encomiums*, to this Lord, or that Lady, who ſtood in need of ſuch triffling merchandiſe. You ſee, my Lord, what an awe you have upon me, when I dare not offer you that incenſe, which wou'd be acceptable to other Patrons: but am forc'd to curb my ſelf, from aſcribing to you thoſe honours, which even an Enemy cou'd not deny you. Yet I muſt confeſs I never practis'd that virtue of moderation *(* which is properly your Character *)* with ſo much reluctancy as now. For it hinders me from being true to my own knowledge, in not witneſſing your worth; and deprives me of the only means which I had left to ſhew the world that true honour and unintereſſed reſpect which I have always payed you. I would ſay ſomewhat, if it were poſſible, which might diſtinguiſh that veneration I have for you, from the flatteries of thoſe who adore your fortune. But the eminence of your condition, in this particular, is my unhappineſs: for it renders whatever I would ſay ſuſpected. Profeſſions of Service, ſubmiſſions, and attendance, are the practiſe of all men to the great: and commonly they who have the leaſt ſincerity, perform them beſt; as they who are leaſt ingag'd in love, have their tongues the freeſt to counterfeit a paſſion: for my own part, I never cou'd ſhake off the ruſtique baſhfulneſs which hangs upon my nature; but valluing my ſelf, at as little as I am worth, have been affraid to render even the common duties of reſpect to thoſe who are in power. The Ceremonious viſits which are generally payed on ſuch occaſions, are not my tallent. They may be real even in Courtiers; but they appear with ſuch a face of intereſt, that a modeſt man wou'd think himſelf in danger of having his ſincerity miſtaken for his deſign. My congratulations keep their diſtance, and paſs no farther than my heart. There it is, that I have all the joy imaginable when I ſee true worth rewarded; and virtue uppermoſt in the world.

If therefore there were one to whom I had the honour to be known; and to know him ſo perfectly, that I could ſay without flattery, he had all the depth of underſtanding that was requiſite in any able Stateſman, and all that honeſty which commonly is wanting; that he was brave without vanity, and knowing without poſitiveneſs: that he was loyall to his Prince, and a lover of his Country; that his principles were full of moderation, and all his Councils ſuch as tended to heal and not to widen the breaches of the Nation: that in all his converſation there appear'd a native candour, and a deſire of doing good in all his actions; if ſuch

an

an one whom I have deſcrib'd, were at the helm, if he had riſen by his merits, and were choſen out in the neceſſity and preſſure of affairs, to remedy our confuſions by the ſeaſonableneſs of his advice, and to put a ſtop to our ruine, when we were juſt rowling downward to the precipice, I ſhou'd then congratulate the Age in which I liv'd, for the common ſafety; I ſhould not deſpair of the Republique though *Hannibal* were at the gates; I ſhould ſend up my vows for the ſucceſs of ſuch an action as *Virgil* did on the like occaſion for his Patron, when he was raiſing up his country from the deſolations of a civill war.

> *Hunc ſaltem everſo juvenem ſuccurrere ſeclo,*
> *Ne ſuperi prohibete.*

I know not whether I am running, in this extaſy which is now upon me: I am almoſt ready to reaſſume the ancient rights of Poetry; to point out, and Prophecy the man, who was born for no leſſe an undertaking; and whom poſterity ſhall bleſs for its accompliſhment. Methinks I am already taking fire from ſuch a Character, and making room for him, under a borrow'd name amongſt the Heroes of an *Epique* Poem. Neither could mine, or ſome more happy Genius, want encouragement under ſuch a Patron.

> *Pollio amat noſtram, quamvis ſit ruſtica Muſam.*

But theſe are conſiderations afar off my Lord: the former part of the Prophecy muſt be firſt accompliſh'd: the quiet of the Nation muſt be ſecur'd; and a mutuall truſt, betwixt Prince and people be renew'd: and then this great and good man will have leiſure for the ornaments of peace: and make our language as much indebted to his care, as the French is to the memorie of their famous *Richelieu*. You know My Lord, how low he lay'd the foundations of ſo great a work: That he began it with a *Grammar* and a *Dictionary*; without which all thoſe Remarques and Obſervations, which have ſince been made, had been perform'd to as little purpoſe as it wou'd be to conſider the furniture of the Rooms before the contrivance of the Houſe. Propriety muſt firſt be ſtated, ere any meaſures of elegance can be taken. Neither is one *Vaugelas* ſufficient for ſuch a work. 'Twas the employment of the whole Academy for many years, for the perfect knowledge of a Tongue, was never attain'd by any ſingle perſon. The Court, the Colledge, and the Town, muſt be joyn'd in it. And as our Engliſh is a compoſition of the dead and living Tongues, there is requir'd a
perfect

perfect knowledge, not onely of the Greek and Latine, but of the Old German, the French and the Italian : and to help all thefe, a converfation with thofe Authours of our own, who have written with the feweft faults in profe and verfe. But how barbaroufly we yet write and fpeak, your Lordfhip knows, and I am fufficiently fenfible in my own Englifh. For I am often put to a ftand, in confidering whether what I write be the Idiom of the Tongue, or falfe *Grammar*, and nonfence couch'd beneath that fpecious Name of *Anglicifme*. And have no other way to clear my doubts, but by tranflating my Englifh into Latine, and thereby trying what fence the words will bear in a more ftable language. I am defirous if it were poffible, that we might all write with the fame certainty of words and purity of phrafe, to which the Italians firft arriv'd, and after them the French : At leaft that we might advance fo far, as our Tongue is capable of fuch a ftandard. It wou'd mortify an Englifh man to confider, that from the time of *Boccace* and of *Petrarche*, the Italian has varied very little : And that the Englifh of *Chaucer* their contemporary is not to be underftood without the help of an Old *Dictionary*. But their Goth and Vandall had the fortune to be graffed on a Roman ftock : Ours has the difadvantage, to be founded on the Dutch. We are full of Monofyllables, and thofe clog'd with confonants, and our pronunciation is effeminate. All which are enemies to a fonnding language : 'Tis true that to fupply our poverty, we have trafficqued with our Neighbour Nations ; by which means we abound as much in words, as *Amfterdam* does in Religions ; but to order them, and make them ufefull after their admiffion is the difficulty. A greater progrefs has been made in this, fince his Majefties return, then perhaps fince the conqueft to his time. But the better part of the work remains unfinifh'd : And that which has been done already, fince it has only been in the practife of fome few writers, muft be digefted into Rules and Method ; before it can be profitable to the General. Will your Lordfhip give me leave to fpeak out at laft ? and to acquaint the world, that from your encouragement and patronage, we may one day expect to fpeak and write a language, worthy of the Englifh wit, and which foreigners may not difdain to learn. Your birth, your Education, your naturall endowments, the former Employments which you have had abroad, and that which to the joy of good men you now exercife at home, feem all to confpire to this defign : the Genius of the Nation feems to call you out as it were by name, to polifh and adorn your native language, and to take from it the reproach of its barbarity. 'Tis upon this encouragement that I have adventur d

The Epiftle Dedicatory.

tur'd on the following Critique, which I humbly prefent you together with the Play : In which, though I have not had the leifure, nor indeed the encouragement to proceed to the Principal
Subject of it, which is the words and thoughts that are futable
to Tragedie ; yet the whole difcourfe has a tendency that
way, and is preliminary to it. In what I have already done, I
doubt not but I have contradicted fome of my former opinions,
in my loofe Effays of the like nature : but of this, I dare af-
firm, that it is the fruit of my riper age and experience, and
that felf-love, or envy have no part in it. The application to
Englifh Anthours is my own, and therein perhaps I may have
err'd unknowingly : But the foundation of the rules is reafon, and
the authority of thofe living Critiques who have had the honour
to be known to you abroad, as well as of the Ancients, who are
not leffe of your acquaintance. Whatfoever it be, I fubmit it to
your Lordfhips Judgment, from which I never will appeal, un-
leffe it be to your good nature, and your candour. If you can
allow an hour of leifure to the perufal of it, I fhall be fortunate
that I cou'd fo long entertain you ; if not, I fhall at leaft have
the fatisfaction to know, that your time was more ufefully employ'd
upon the publique. I am,

My Lord,

Your Lordfhips moft Obedier

Humble Servant,

John Dryden.

The PREFACE to the Play.

THe Poet Æſchylus *was held in the ſame veneration by the Athenians of after Ages as* Shakeſpear *is by us*; *and* Longinus *has judg'd, in favour of him, that he had a noble boldneſſe of expreſſion, and that his imaginations were lofty and Heroick*: *but on the other ſide* Quintilian *affirms, that he was daring to extravagance.* 'Tis *certain, that he affected pompous words, and that his ſence too often was obſcur'd by Figures*: *Notwithſtanding theſe imperfections, the value of his Writings after his deceaſe was ſuch, that his Countrymen ordain'd an equal reward to thoſe Poets who could alter his Plays to be Acted on the Theater, with thoſe whoſe productions were wholly new, and of their own. The caſe is not the ſame in* England; *though the difficulties of altering are greater, and our reverence for* Shakeſpear *much more juſt, then that of the* Grecians *for* Æſchylus. *In the Age of that Poet, the* Greek *tongue was arriv'd to its full perfection*; *they had then amongſt them an exact Standard of Writing, and of Speaking*: *The* Engliſh *Language is not capable of ſuch a certainty*; *and we are at preſent ſo far from it, that we are wanting in the very Foundation of it, a perfect Grammar. Yet it muſt be allow'd to the preſent Age, that the tongue in general is ſo much refin'd ſince* Shakeſpear's *time, that many of his words, and more of his Phraſes, are ſcarce intelligible. And of thoſe which we underſtand ſome are ungrammatical, others courſe*; *and his whole ſtile is ſo peſter'd with Figurative expreſſions, that it is as affected as it is obſcure.* 'Tis *true, that in his later Plays he had worn off ſomewhat of the ruſt*; *but the Tragedy which I have undertaken to correct, was, in all probability, one of his firſt endeavours on the Stage.*

The Original ſtory was Written by one Lollius *a* Lombard, *in* Latin *verſe, and Tranſlated by* Chaucer *into* Engliſh: *intended I ſuppoſe a Satyr on the Inconſtancy of Women: I find nothing of it among the Ancients; not ſo much as the name once* Creſſida *mention'd.* Shakeſpear, (*as I hinted*) *in the Aprenticeſhip of his Writing, model'd it into that Play, which is now call'd by the name of* Troilus *and* Creſſida; *but ſo lamely is it left to us, that it is not divided into Acts: which fault I aſcribe to the Actors, who Printed it after* Shakeſpear's *death*; *and that too, ſo careleſly, that a more uncorrect Copy I never ſaw. For the Play it ſelf, the Author ſeems to have begun it with ſome fire*; *the Characters of* Pandarus *and* Therſites, *are promiſing enough*; *but as if he grew weary of his task, after an Entrance or two, he lets 'em fall: and the later part of the Tragedy is nothing but a confuſion of Drums and Trumpets, Excurſions and Alarms. The chief perſons, who give name to the Tragedy, are left alive:* Creſſida *is falſe, and is not puniſh'd. Yet after all, becauſe the Play was* Shakeſpear's, *and that there appear'd in ſome places of it, the admirable Genius of the Author*; *I undertook to remove that heap of Rubbiſh, under which many excellent thoughts lay wholly bury'd. Accordingly, I new model'd the Plot*; *threw out many unneceſſary perſons*; *improv'd thoſe Characters*

racters

racters which were begun, and left unfinish'd: as Hector, Troilus, Pandarus *and* Thersites ; *and added that of* Andromache. *After this, I made
with no small trouble, an Order and Connexion of all the Scenes ; removing
them from the places where they were inartificially set : and though it was im-
possible to keep 'em all unbroken, because the Scene must be sometimes in the City,
and sometimes in the Camp, yet I have so order'd them that there is a coherence
of 'em with one another, and a dependence on the main design : no leaping from*
Troy *to the Grecian Tents, and thence back again in the same Act ; but a due
proportion of time allow'd for every motion. I need not say that I have refin'd
his Language, which before was obsolete; but I am willing to acknowledg, that as
I have often drawn his* English *nearer to our times so I have somtimes conform'd
my own to his: & consequently, the Language is not altogether so pure, as it is sig-
nificant. The Scenes of* Pandarus *and* Cressida, *of* Troilus *and* Pandarus, *of*
Andromache *with* Hector *and the Trojans, in the second Act, are wholly*
New : *together with that of* Nestor *and* Ulysses *with* Thersites ; *and that
of* Thersites *with* Ajax *and* Achilles. *I will not weary my Reader with the
Scenes which are added of* Pandarus *and the Lovers, in the Third ; and those
of* Thersites, *which are wholly alter'd : but I cannot omit the last Scene in it,
which is almost half the Act, betwixt* Troilus *and* Hector. *The occasion of
raising it was hinted to me by Mr.* Betterton : *the contrivance and
working of it was my own. They who think to do me an injury, by saying that
it is an imitation of the Scene betwixt* Brutus *and* Cassius, *do me an honour, by
supposing I could imitate the incomparable* Shakespear : *but let me add, that if*
Shakespears *Scene, or that faulty Copy of it in* Amintor *and* Melantius *had
never been, yet* Euripides *had furnish'd me with an excellent example in his*
Iphigenia, *between* Agamemnon *and* Menelaus : *and from thence indeed,
the last turn of it is borrow'd. The occasion which* Shakespear, Euripides, *and*
Fletcher, *have all taken, is the same ; grounded upon Friendship : and the
quarrel of two virtuous men, rais'd by natural degrees, to the extremity of passion, is conducted in all three, to the declination of the same passion ; and con-
cludes with a warm renewing of their Friendship. But the particular ground-
work which* Shakespear *has taken, is incomparably the best : Because he has
not only chosen two the greatest Heroes of their Age ; but has likewise interested
the Liberty of* Rome, *and their own honors, who were the redeemers of it, in this
debate. And if he has made* Brutus *who was naturally a patient man, to fly
into excess at first ; let it be remembred in his defence, that just before, he has receiv'd the news of* Portia's *death : whom the Poet on purpose neglecting a little
Chronology, supposes to have dy'd before* Brutus, *only to give him an occasion
of being more easily exasperated. Add to this, that the injury he had receiv'd
from* Cassius, *had long been brooding in his mind ; and that a melancholy man,
upon consideration of an affront, especially from a Friend, would be more eager
in his passion, than he who had given it, though naturally more cholerick.* Euripides *whom I have follow'd, has rais'd the quarrel betwixt two Brothers
who were friends. The foundation of the Scene was this : The* Grecians *were
wind-bound at the Port of* Aulis, *and the Oracle had said, that they could not*

The Preface.

Sail, *unless* Agamemnon *deliver'd up his Daughter to be Sacrific'd: he refuses*; *his Brother* Menelaus *urges the publick safety, the Father defends himself, by arguments of natural affection, and hereupon they quarrel.* Agamemnon *is at last convinc'd, and promises to deliver up* Iphigenia, *but so passionately laments his loss, that* Menelaus *is griev'd to have been the occasion of it, and by a return of kindness, offers to intercede for him with the* Grecians, *that his Daughter might not be sacrific'd. But my friend Mr.* Rymer *has so largly, and with so much judgement describ'd this Scene, in comparing it with that of* Melantius *and* Amintor, *that it is superfluous to say more of it : I only nam'd the heads of it, that any reasonable man might judge it was from thence I model'd my Scene betwixt* Troilus *and* Hector. *I will conclude my reflexions on it, with a passage of* Longinus, *concerning* Plato's *imitation of* Homer :* 'We ought not to regard a good imitation as a theft ; but as a beautifull
'Idea of him who undertakes to imitate, by forming himself on the invention and
'the work of another man; for he enters into the lists like a new wrestler, to dis-
'pute the prize with the former Champion. This sort of emulation says* Hesiod,
'*is honourable* Ἀγαθὴ δ᾽ ἔρις ἐςὶ βροǀιοισιν --- When we combat for Victory with
'a Hero, and are not without glory even in our overthrow. Those great men
'whom we propose to our selves as patterns of our imitation, serve us as a Torch,
'which is lifted up before us, to enlighten our passage ; and often elevate our
'thoughts as high, as the conception we have of our Authors Genius.*

I have been so tedious in three *Acts, that I shall contract my self in the two last. The beginning Scenes of the fourth Act are either added, or chang'd wholly by me ; the middle of it is* Shakespear *alter'd, and mingled with my own, three or four of the last Scenes are altogether new. And the whole Fifth Act, both the Plot and the Writing are my own Additions.*

But having written so much for imitation of what is excellent, in that part of the Preface which related only to my self ; methinks it would neither be unprofitable nor unpleasant to enquire how far we ought to imitate our own Poets, Shakespear *and* Fletcher *in their Tragedies : And this will occasion another enquiry, how those two Writers differ between themselves : but since neither of these questions can be solv'd unless some measures be first taken, by which we may be enabled to judge truly of their Writings : I shall endeavour as briefly as I can, to discover the grounds and reason of all Criticism, applying them in this place only to Tragedy.* Aristotle *with his Interpreters, and* Horace, *and* Longinus, *are the Authors to whom I owe my lights ; and what part soever of my own Plays, or of this, which no mending could make regular, shall fall under the condemnation of such Judges, it would be impudence in me to defend. I think it no shame to retract my errors, and am well pleas'd to suffer in the cause, if the Art may be improv'd at my expence : I therefore proceed to,*

The Grounds of Criticism in Tragedy.

TRagedy *is thus defin'd by* Aristotle, (*omiting what I thought unnecessary in his Definition.*) '*Tis an imitation of one intire, great, and probable action ; not told but represented, which by moving in us fear and pity, is
conducive*

The Preface.

conducive to the purging of those two passions in our minds. More largely thus, Tragedy describes or paints an Action, which Action must have all the proprieties above nam'd. First, it must be one or single, that is, it must not be a History of one Mans life: Suppose of Alexander the Great, or Julius Cæsar, but one single action of theirs. This condemns all Shakespears Historical Plays, which are rather Chronicles represented, than Tragedies, and all double action of Plays. As to avoid a Satyr upon others, I will make bold with my own Marriage-A-la-Mode, where there are manifestly two Actions, not depending on one another: but in Oedipus there cannot properly be said to be two Actions, because the love of Adrastus and Euridice has a necessary dependance on the principal design, into which it is woven. The natural reason of this Rule is plain, for two different independant actions, distract the attention and concernment of the Audience, and consequently destroy the intention of the Poet: If his business be to move terror and pity, and one of his Actions be Comical, the other Tragical, the former will divert the people, and utterly make void his greater purpose. Therefore as in Perspective, so in Tragedy, there must be a point of sight in which all the lines terminate: Otherwise the eye wanders, and the work is false. This was the practice of the Grecian Stage. But Terence made an innovation in the Roman: all his Plays have double Actions; for it was his custome to Translate two Greek Comedies, and to weave them into one of his, yet so, that both the Actions were Comical; and one was principal, the other but secondary or subservient. And this has obtain'd on the English Stage, to give us the pleasure of variety.

As the Action ought to be one, it ought as such, to have Order in it, that is, to have a natural beginning, a middle, and an end: A natural beginning says Aristotle, is that which could not necessarily have been plac'd after another thing, and so of the rest. This consideration will arraign all Plays after the new model of Spanish Plots, where accident is heap'd upon accident, and that which is first might as reasonably be last: an inconvenience not to be remedyed, but by making one accident naturally produce another, otherwise 'tis a Farce, and not a Play. Of this nature, is the Slighted Maid; where there is no Scene in the first Act, which might not by as good reason be in the fifth. And if the Action ought to be one, the Tragedy ought likewise to conclude with the Action of it. Thus in Mustapha, the Play should naturally have ended with the death of Zanger, and not have given us the grace Cup after Dinner, of Solyman's divorce from Roxolana.

The following properties of the Action are so easy, that they need not my explaining. It ought to be great, and to consist of great Persons, to distinguish it from Comedy; where the Action is trivial, and the persons of inferior rank. The last quality of the action is, that it ought to be probable, as well as admirable and great. 'Tis not necessary that there should be Historical truth in it; but always necessary that there should be a likeness of truth, something that is more then barely possible, probable being that which succeeds or happens oftner than it misses. To invent therefore a probability, and to make it wonderfull, is the most difficult undertaking in the Art of Poetry: for that which is not won-

derfull,

The Preface.

derfull, is not great, and that which is not probable, will not delight a reasonable Audience. This action thus describ'd, must be represented and not told, to distinguish Dramatic Poetry from Epic: but I hasten to the end, or scope of Tragedy; which is to rectify or purge our passions, fear and pity.

To instruct delightfully is the general end of all Poetry: Philosophy instructs, but it performs its work by precept: which is not delightfull, or not so delightfull as Example. To purge the passions by Example, is therefore the particular instruction which belongs to Tragedy. Rapin a judicious Critic, has observ'd from Aristotle, that pride and want of commiseration are the most predominant vices in Mankinde: therefore to cure us of these two, the inventors of Tragedy, have chosen to work upon two other passions, which are fear and pity. We are wrought to fear, by their seting before our eyes some terrible example of misfortune, which hapned to persons of the highest Quality; for such an action demonstrates to us, that no condition is privileg'd from the turns of Fortune: this must of necessity cause terror in us, and consequently abate our pride. But when we see that the most virtuous, as well as the greatest, are not exempt from such misfortunes, that consideration moves pity in us: and insensibly works us to be helpfull to, and tender over the distress'd, which is the noblest and most God-like of moral virtues. Here 'tis observable, that it is absolutely neccessary to make a man virtuous, if we desire he should be pity'd: We lament not, but detest a wicked man, we are glad when we behold his crimes are punish'd, and that Poetical justice is done upon him. Euripides was censur'd by the Critics of his time, for making his chief characters too wicked: for example, Phaedra though she lov'd her Son-in-law with reluctancy, and that it was a curse upon her Family for offending Venus; yet was thought too ill a pattern for the Stage. Shall we therefore banish all characters of villany? I confess I am not of that opinion; but it is neccessary that the Hero of the Play be not a Villain: that is, the characters which should move our pity ought to have virtuous inclinations, and degrees of morall goodness in them. As for a perfect character of virtue, it never was in Nature; and therefore there can be no imitation of it: but there are allays of frailty to be allow'd for the chief Persons, yet so that the good which is in them, shall outweigh the bad; and consequently leave room for punishment on the one side, and pity on the other.

After all, if any one will ask me, whether a Tragedy cannot be made upon any other grounds, than those of exciting pity and terror in us? Bossu, the best of modern Critics, answers thus in general: That all excellent Arts, and particularly that of Poetry, have been invented and brought to perfection by men of a transcendent Genius; and that therefore they who practice afterwards the same Arts, are oblig'd to tread in their footsteps, and to search in their Writings the foundation of them: for it is not just that new Rules should destroy the authority of the old. But Rapin writes more particularly thus: That no passions in a story are so proper to move our concernment as Fear and Pity; and that it is from our concernment we receive our pleasure, is undoubted; when the Soul becomes agitated with fear for one character, or hope for another; then it is that we are pleas'd in Tragedy, by the interest which we take in their adventures.

Here

The Preface.

Here therefore the general answer may be given to the first question, how far we ought to imitate Shakespear and Fletcher in their Plots; namely that we ought to follow them so far only, as they have Copy'd the excellencies of those who invented and brought to perfection Dramatic Poetry: those things only excepted which Religion, customs of Countries, Idioms of Languages, &c. have alter'd in the Superstructures, but not in the foundation of the design.

How defective Shakespear and Fletcher have been in all their Plots, Mr. Rymer has discover'd in his Criticisms: neither can we, who follow them, be excus'd from the same or greater errors; which are the more unpardonable in us, because we want their beauties to counterveil our faults. The best of their designs, the most approaching to Antiquity, and the most conducing to move pity, is the King and no King; which if the Farce of Bessus were thrown away, is of that inferior sort of Tragedies, which end with a prosprous event. 'Tis probably deriv'd from the story of OEdipus, with the character of Alexander the Great, in his extravagancies, given to Arbaces. The taking of this Play, amongst many others, I cannot wholly ascribe to the excellency of the action; for I finde it moving when it is read: 'tis true, the faults of the Plot are so evidently prov'd, that they can no longer be deny'd. The beauties of it must therefore lie either in the lively touches of the passions: or we must conclude, as I think we may, that even in imperfect Plots, there are less degrees of Nature, by which some faint emotions of pity and terror are rais'd in us: as a less Engine will raise a less proportion of weight, though not so much as one of Archimedes making; for nothing can move our nature, but by some natural reason, which works upon passions. And since we acknowledge the effect, there must be something in the cause.

The difference between Shakespear and Fletcher in their Plotting seems to be this; that Shakespear generally moves more terror, and Fletcher more compassion: For the first had a more Masculine, a bolder and more fiery Genius; the Second a more soft and Womanish. In the mechanic beauties of the Plot, which are the Observation of the three Unities, Time, Place, and Action, they are both deficient; but Shakespear most. Ben. Johnson reform'd those errors in his Comedies, yet one of Shakespear's was Regular before him: which is, The Merry Wives of Windsor. For what remains concerning the design, you are to be refer'd to our English Critic. That method which he has prescrib'd to raise it from mistake, or ignorance of the crime, is certainly the best though 'tis not the only: for amongst all the Tragedies of Sophocles, there is but one, OEdipus, which is wholly built after that model.

After the Plot, which is the foundation of the Play, the next thing to which we ought to apply our Judgment is the manners, for now the Poet comes to work above ground: the ground-work indeed is that which is most necessary, as that upon which depends the firmness of the whole Fabric; yet it strikes not the eye so much, as the beauties or imperfections of the manners, the thoughts and the expressions.

The first Rule which Bossu, prescribes to the Writer of an Heroic Poem, and which holds too by the same reason in all Dramatic Poetry, is to make the

moral

moral of the work ; that is, to lay down to your self what that precept of morality shall be, which you would insinuate into the people : as namely, Homer's, (which I have Copy'd in my Conquest of Granada *) was, that Union preserves a Common-wealth, and discord destroys it.* Sophocles, *in his* Œdipus, *that no man is to be accounted happy before his death. 'Tis the Moral that directs the whole action of the* Play *to one center ; and that action or Fable, is the example built upon the moral, which confirms the truth of it to our experience : when the Fable is design'd, then and not before, the Persons are to be introduc'd with their manners, characters and passions.*

The manners in a Poem, are understood to be those inclinations, whether natural or acquir'd, which move and carry us to actions, good, bad, or indifferent in a Play ; or which incline the persons to such, or such actions : I have anticipated part of this discourse already, in declaring that a Poet ought not to make the manners perfectly good in his best persons, but neither are they to be more wicked in any of his characters, than necessity requires. To produce a Villain, without other reason than a natural inclination to villany, is in Poetry to produce an effect without a cause : and to make him more a Villain than he has just reason to be, is to make an effect which is stronger then the cause.

The manners arise from many causes : and are either distinguish'd by complexion, as choleric and phlegmatic, or by the differences of Age or Sex, of Climates, or Quality of the persons, or their present condition : they are likewise to be gather'd from the several Virtues, Vices, or Passions, and many other common-places which a Poet must be suppos'd to have learn'd from natural Philosophy, Ethics, and History ; of all which whosoever is ignorant, does not deserve the Name of Poet.

But as the manners are usefull in this Art, they may be all compris'd under these general heads : First, they must be apparent, that is in every character of the Play, some inclinations of the Person must appear : and these are shown in the actions and discourse. Secondly the manners must be suitable or agreeing to the Persons ; that is, to the Age, Sex, dignity, and the other general heads of Manners : thus when a Poet has given the Dignity of a King to one of his persons, in all his actions and speeches, that person must discover Majesty, Magnanimity, and jealousy of power ; because these are sutable to the general manners of a King. The third property of manners is resemblance; and this is founded upon the particular characters of men, as we have them deliver'd to us by relation or History : that is, when a Poet has the known character of this or that man before him, he is bound to represent him such, at least not contrary to that which Fame has reported him to have been : thus it is not a Poets choice to make Ulysses *choleric, or* Achilles *patient, because* Homer *has describ'd 'em quite otherwise. Yet this is a Rock, on which ignorant Writers daily split : and the absurdity is as monstrous, as if a Painter should draw a Coward running from a Battle, and tell us it was the Picture of* Alexander *the Great.*

The last property of manners is, that they be constant, and equal, that is, maintain'd the same through the whole design : thus when Virgil *had once given the name of* Pious *to* Æneas, *he was bound to show him such, in all his*
words

The Preface.

words and actions through the whole Poem. All these properties Horace *has hinted to a judicious observer.* 1. Notandi sunt tibi mores, 2. aut famam sequere, 3. aut sibi convenientia finge. 4. Servetur ad imum, qualis ab incœpto processerat, & sibi constet.

From the manners, the Characters of persons are deriv'd, for indeed the characters are no other than the inclinations, as they appear in the several persons of the Poem. A character being thus defin'd, that which distinguishes one man from another. Not to repeat the same things over again which have been said of the manners, I will only add what is necessary here. A character, or that which distinguishes one man from all others, cannot be suppos'd to consist of one particular Virtue, or Vice, or passion only ; but 'tis a composition of qualities which are not contrary to one another in the same person : thus the same man may be liberal and valiant, but not liberal and covetous ; so in a Comical character, or humour, (which is an inclination to this, or that particular folly) Falstaff is a lyar, and a coward, a Glutton, and a Buffon, because all these qualities may agree in the same man ; yet it is still to be observ'd, that one virtue, vice, and passion, ought to be shown in every man, as predominant over all the rest : as covetousness in Crassus, love of his Country in Brutus ; and the same in characters which are feign'd.

The chief character or Hero in a Tragedy, as I have already shown, ought in prudence to be such a man, who has so much more in him of Virtue than of Vice, that he may be left amiable to the Audience, which otherwise cannot have any concernment for his sufferings : and 'tis on this one character that the pity and terror must be principally, if not wholly founded. A Rule which is extreamly necessary, and which none of the Criticks that I know, have fully enough discover'd to us. For terror and compassion work but weakly, when they are divided into many persons. If Creon had been the chief character in OEdipus, *there had neither been terror nor compassion mov'd ; but only detestation of the man and joy for his punishment ; if* Adrastus *and* Euridice *had been made more appearing characters, then the pity had been divided, and lessen'd on the part of* OEdipus : *but making* OEdipus *the best and bravest person, and even* Jocasta *but an underpart to him ; his virtues and the punishment of his fatall crime, drew both the pity, and the terror to himself.*

By what had been said of the manners, it will be easy for a reasonable man to judge, whether the characters be truly or falsely drawn in a Tragedy ; for if there be no manners appearing in the characters, no concernment for the persons can be rais'd : no pity or horror can be mov'd, but by vice or virtue, therefore without them, no person can have any business in the Play. If the inclinations be obscure, 'tis a sign the Poet is in the dark, and knows not what manner of man he presents to you ; and consequently you can have no Idea, or very imperfect, of that man : nor can judge what resolutions he ought to take ; or what words or actions are proper for him : Most Comedies made up of accidents, or adventures, are liable to fall into this error : and Tragedies with many turns are subject to it : for the manners never can be evident, where the surprises of Fortune take up all the business of the Stage ; and where the Poet *is*

more

more in pain, to tell you what hapned to such a man, than what he was. 'Tis one of the excellencies of Shakespear, *that the manners of his persons are generally apparent ; and you see their bent and inclinations.* Fletcher *comes far short of him in this, as indeed he does almost in every thing : there are but glimmerings of manners in most of his Comedies, which run upon adventures : and in his Tragedies,* Rollo, Otto, *the* King and No King, Melantius, *and many others of his best, are but Pictures shown you in the twi-light ; you know not whether they resemble vice, or virtue, and they are either good bad, or indifferent, as the present Scene requires it. But of all Poets, this commendation is to be given to* Ben. Johnson, *that the manners even of the most inconsiderable persons in his Plays are every where apparent.*

By considering the Second quality of manners, which is that they be sutable to the Age, Quality, Country, Dignity, &c. of the character, we may likewise judge whether a Poet has follow'd Nature. In this kinde Sophocles *and* Euripides, *have more excell'd among the Greeks than* Æschylus *: and* Terence, *more then* Plautus *among the Romans : Thus* Sophocles *gives to* OEdipus *the true qualities of a King, in both those Plays which bear his Name : but in the latter which is the* OEdipus Colonœus, *he lets fall on purpose his Tragic Stile, his Hero speaks not in the Arbitrary tone ; but remembers in the softness of his complaints, that he is an unfortunate blind Old-man, that he is banish'd from his Country, and persecuted by his next Relations. The present French Poets are generally accus'd, that wheresoever they lay the Scene, or in whatsoever Age, the manners of their Heroes are wholly French :* Racin's Bajazet *is bred at* Constantinople *; but his civilities are convey'd to him by some secret passage, from* Versailles *into the Seraglio. But our* Shakespear, *having ascrib'd to* Henry the Fourth *the character of a King, and of a Father, gives him the perfect manners of each Relation, when either he transacts with his Son, or with his Subjects.* Fletcher, *on the other side gives neither to* Arbaces, *nor to his King in the* Maids Tragedy, *the qualities which are sutable to a Monarch : though he may be excus'd a little in the latter ; for the King there is not uppermost in the character ; 'tis the Lover of* Evadne, *who is King only, in a second consideration ; and though he be unjust, and has other faults which shall be nameless, yet he is not the Hero of the Play : 'tis true we finde him a lawfull Prince, (though I never heard of any King that was in* Rhodes *) and therefore Mr.* Rymers *Criticism stands good ; that he should not be shown in so vicious a character.* Sophocles *has been more judicious in his* Antigona *for though he represent in* Creon *a bloody Prince, yet he makes him not a lawful King, but an Usurper, and* Antigona *her self is the Heroin of the Tragedy : But when* Philaster *wounds* Arethusa *and the Boy ; and* Perigot *his Mistress, in the faithfull* Sheperdess, *both these are contrary to the character of Manhood : Nor is* Valentinian *manag'd much better, for though* Fletcher *has taken his Picture truly, and shown him as he was, an effeminate voluptuous man, yet he has forgotten that he was an Emperor, and has given him none of those Royal marks, which ought to appear in a lawfull Successor of the Throne. If it be enquir'd, what* Fletcher *should have done on this occasion ; ought he not to have*
represented

The Preface.

represented Valentinian *as he was?* Boffu *fhall anfwer this queftion for me,
by an inftance of the like nature :* Mauritius *the Greek Emperor, was a Prince
far furpaffing* Valentinian, *for he was indued with many Kingly virtues ; he
was Religious, Mercifull, and Valiant, but withall he was noted of extream
covetoufnefs, a vice which is contrary to the character of a Hero, or a Prince:
therefore fays the Critic, that Emperor was no fit perfon to be reprefented in a
Tragedy, unlefs his good qualities were only to be fhown, and his covetoufnefs
(which fullyed them all) were flur'd over by the artifice of the Poet. To return
once more to* Shakefpear ; *no man ever drew fo many characters, or general'y
diftinguifhed'em better from one another, excepting only* Johnfon : *I will inftance but in one, to fhow the copioufnefs of his Invention ; 'tis that of* Calyban,
or the Monfter in the Tempeft. *He feems there to have created a perfon which
was not in Nature, a boldnefs which at firft fight would appear intolerable : for
he makes him a Species of himfelf, begotten by an* Incubus *on a Witch ; but
this as I have elfewhere prov'd, is not wholly beyond the bounds of credibility,
at leaft the vulgar ftile believe it. We have the feparated notions of a fpirit,
and of a Witch; (and Spirits according to* Plato, *are vefted with a fubtil body ;
according to fome of his followers, have different Sexes) therefore as from
the diftinct apprehenfions of a Horfe, and of a Man, Imagination has form'd
a* Centaur, *fo from thofe of an* Incubus *and a Sorcerefs,* Shakefpear *has
produc'd his Monfter. Whether or no his Generation can be defended, I leave
to Philofophy; but of this I am certain, that the Poet has moft judicioufly fur-
nifh'd him with a perfon, a Language, and a character, which will fuit him,
both by Fathers and Mothers fide : he has all the difcontents, and malice of a
Witch, and of a Devil ; befides a convenient proportion of the deadly fins ;
Gluttory, Sloth, and Luft, are manifeft ; the dejectednefs of a flave is like-
wife given him, and the ignorance of one bred up in a Defart Ifland. His perfon is monftrous, as he is the product of unnatural Luft ; and his language is
as hobgoblin as his perfon : in all things he is diftinguifh'd from other mortals.
The characters of* Fletcher *are poor & narrow, in comparifon of* Shakefpears;
*I remember not one which is not borrow'd from him ; unlefs you will except that
ftrange mixture of a man in the* King and no King : *So that in this part*
Shakefpear *is generally worth our Imitation ; and to imitate* Fletcher *is but
to Copy after him who was a Copyer.*

*Under this general head of Manners, the paffions are naturally included, as
belonging to the Characters. I fpeak not of pity and of terror, which are to be
mov'd in the Audience by the Plot ; but of Anger, Hatred, Love, Ambition,
Jealoufy, Revenge, &c. as they are fhown in this or that perfon of the* Play.
*To defcribe thefe naturally, and to move them artfully, is one of the greateft
commendations which can be given to a Poet : to write pathetically, fays* Longinus, *cannot proceed but for a lofty* Genius. *A Poet muft be born with this
quality ; yet, unlefs he help himfelf by an acquir'd knowledg of the Paffions,
what they are in their own nature, and by what fprings they are to be mov'd,
he will be fubject either to raife them where they ought not to be rais'd, or not to
raife them by the juft degrees of Nature, or to amplify them beyond the natural*

bounds

bounds, or not to observe the crisis and turns of them, in their cooling and decay: all which errors proceed from want of Judgment in the Poet, and from being unskill'd in the Principles of Moral Philosophy. Nothing is more frequent in a Fanciful Writer, than to foil himself by not managing his strength: therefore, as in a Wrestler, there is first requir'd some measure of force, a well-knit body, and active Limbs, without which all instruction would be vain; yet, these being granted, if he want the skill which is necessary to a Wrestler, he shall make but small advantage of his natural robustuousness: So in a Poet, his inborn vehemence and force of spirit, will only run him out of breath the sooner, if it be not supported by the help of Art. The roar of passion indeed may please an Audience, three parts of which are ignorant enough to think all is moving which is noise, and it may stretch the lungs of an ambitious Actor, who will dye upon the spot for a thundring clap; but it will move no other passion than indignation and contempt from judicious men. Longinus, whom I have hitherto follow'd, continues thus: If the passions be Artfully employ'd, the discourse becomes vehement and lofty; if otherwise, there is nothing more ridiculous than a great passion out of season: And to this purpose he animadverts severely upon Æschylus, who writ nothing in cold blood, but was always in a rapture, and in fury with his Audience: the Inspiration was still upon him, he was ever tearing it upon the Tripos; or (to run off as madly as he does, from one similitude to another) he was always at high floud of Passion, even in the dead Ebb, and lowest Watermark of the Scene. He who would raise the passion of a judicious Audience, says a Learned Critic, must be sure to take his hearers along with him; if they be in a Calm, 'tis in vain for him to be in a huff: he must move them by degrees, and kindle with 'em; otherwise he will be in danger of setting his own heap of Stubble on a fire, and of burning out by himself without warming the company that stand about him. They who would justify the madness of Poetry from the Authority of Aristotle, have mistaken the text, & consequently the Interpretation: I imagine it to be false read, where he says of Poetry, that it is Εὐφυῆς ἢ μανικῦ, that it had always somewhat in it either of a genius, or of a madman. 'Tis more probable that the Original ran thus, that Poetry was Εὐφυῆς ὰ μανικῦ, That it belongs to a Witty man, but not to a madman. Thus then the Passions, as they are consider'd simply and in themselves, suffer violence when they are perpetually maintain'd at the same height; for what melody can be made on that Instrument all whose strings are screw'd up at first to their utmost stretch, and to the same sound? But this is not the worst; for the Characters likewise bear a part in the general calamity, if you consider the Passions as embody'd in them: for it follows of necessity, that no man can be distinguish'd from another by his discourse, when every man is ranting, swaggering, and exclaiming with the same excess: as if it were the only business of all the Characters to contend with each other for the prize at Billingsgate; or that the Scene of the Tragedy lay in Bet'lem. Suppose the Poet should intend this man to be Cholerick, and that man to be patient; yet when they are confounded in the Writing, you cannot distinguish them from one another: for the man who was call'd patient and tame, is only so before he speaks; but let his clack be set a going, and he shall tongue it as

impetuously,

The Preface.

impetuously, and as loudly as the errantest Hero in the Play. By this means, the characters are only distinct in name ; but in reality, all the men and women in the Play are the same person. No man should pretend to write, who cannot temper his fancy with his Judgment : nothing is more dangerous to a raw horse-man, than a hot-mouth'd Jade without a curb.

'Tis necessary therefore for a Poet, who would concern an Audience by describing of a Passion, first to prepare it, and not to rush upon it all at once. Ovid has judiciously shown the difference of these two ways, in the speeches of Ajax and Ulysses : Ajax from the very beginning breaks out into his exclamations, and is swearing by his Maker.——Agimus proh Jupiter inquit. Ulysses on the contrary, prepares his Audience with all the submissivenss he can practice, & all the calmness of a reasonable man ; he found his Judges in a tranquillity of spirit, and therefore set out leasurely and softly with 'em, till he had warm'd 'em by degrees ; and then he began to mend his pace, and to draw them along with his own impetuousness : yet so managing his breath, that it might not fail him at his need, and reserving his utmost proofs of ability even to the last. The success you see was answerable ; for the croud only applauded the speech of Ajax ;——

Vulgique secutum ultima murmur erat :——

But the Judges awarded the prize for which they contended to Ulysses.

Mota manus Procerum est, et quid facundia possit
Tum patuit, fortisque viri arma Disertus.

The next necessary rule is to put nothing into the discourse which may hinder your moving of the passions. Too many accidents as I have said, incomber the Poet, as much as the Arms of Saul did David ; for the variety of passions which they produce, are ever crossing and justling each other out of the way. He who treats of joy and grief together, is in a fair way of causing neither of those effects. There is yet another obstacle to be remov'd, which is pointed Wit, and Sentences affected out of season ; these are nothing of kin to the violence of passion : no man is at leisure to make sentences and similes, when his soul is in an Agony. I the rather name this fault, that it may serve to mind me of my former errors ; neither will I spare my self, but give an example of this kind from my Indian Emperor : Montezuma, pursu'd by his enemies, and seeking Sanctuary, stands parlying without the Fort, and describing his danger to Cydaria, in a simile of six lines ;

As on the sands the frighted Traveller
Sees the high Seas come rowling from afar, &c.

My Indian Potentate was well skill'd in the Sea for an Inland Prince, and well improv'd since the first Act, when he sent his son to discover it. The Image had not been amiss from another man, at another time : Sed nunc non erat hisce locus : he destroy'd the concernment which the Audience might otherwise have had for him ; for they could not think the danger near, when he had the leisure to invent a Simile.

If Shakespear be allow'd, as I think he must, to have made his Characters distinct, it will easily be infer'd that he understood the nature of the Passions : because it has been prov'd already, that confus'd passions make undistingui-

shable

ſhable Characters : yet I cannot deny that he has his failings ; but they are not ſo much in the paſſions themſelves, as in his manner of expreſſion : he of-ten obſcures his meaning by his words, and ſometimes makes it unintelligible. I will not ſay of ſo great a Poet, that he diſtinguiſh'd not the blown puffy ſtile, from true ſublimity ; but I may venture to maintain that the fury of his fancy often tranſported him, beyond the bounds of Judgment, either in coyn-ing of new words and phraſes, or racking words which were in uſe, into the violence of a Catachreſis : 'Tis not that I would explode the uſe of Metaphors from paſſions, for Longinus *thinks 'em neceſſary to raiſe it ; but to uſe 'em at every word, to ſay nothing without a Metaphor, a Simile, an Image, or deſcription, is I doubt to ſmell a little too ſtrongly of the Buskin. I muſt be forc'd to give an example of expreſſing paſſion figuratively ; but that I may do it with reſpect to* Shakeſpear, *it ſhall not be taken from any thing of his : 'tis an exclamation againſt* Fortune, *quoted in his* Hamlet, *but written by ſome other Poet.*

Out, out, thou ſtrumpet fortune ; all you Gods,
In general Synod, take away her Power,
Break all the ſpokes and fallyes from her Wheel,
And bowl the round Nave down the hill of Heav'n
As low as to the Fiends.

And immediately after, ſpeaking of Hecuba, *when* Priam *was kill'd be-fore her eyes :*

The mobbled Queen ran up and down,
Threatning the flame with biſſon rheum : a clout about that head,
Where late the Diadem ſtood ; and for a Robe
About her lank and all o're-teemed loyns,
A blanket in th' alarm of fear caught up.
Who this had ſeen, with tongue in venom ſteep'd
'Gainſt Fortune's ſtate would Treaſon have pronounc'd ;
But if the Gods themſelves did ſee her then,
When ſhe ſaw *Pyrrhus* make malicious ſport
In mincing with his ſword her Husband's Limbs,
The inſtant burſt of clamor that ſhe made
(Unleſs things mortal meant them not at all)
Would have made milch the burning eyes of Heav'n,
And paſſion in the Gods.

What a pudder is here kept in raiſing the expreſſion of trifling thoughts. Would not a man have thought that the Poet had been bound Prentice to a Wheel-wright, for his firſt Rant ? and had follow'd a Ragman, for the clout and blanket, in the ſecond ? Fortune is painted on a wheel ; and therefore the writer in a rage, will have Poetical Juſtice done upon every member of
that

The Preface.

that Engin: after this execution, he bowls the Nave downhill, from Heaven, to the Fiends: (an unreasonable long mark a man would think;) 'tis well there are no solid Orbs to stop it in the way, or no Element of fire to consume it: but when it came to the earth, it must be monstrous heavy, to break ground as low as to the Center. His making milch the burning eyes of Heaven, was a pretty tollerable flight too; and I think no man ever drew milk out of eyes before him: yet to make the wonder greater, these eyes were burning. Such a sight indeed were enough to have rais'd passion in the Gods, but to excuse the effects of it, he tells you perhaps they did not see it. Wise men would be glad to find a little sence couch'd under all those pompous words; for Bombast is commonly the delight of that Audience, which loves Poetry, but understands it not: and as commonly has been the practice of those Writers, who not being able to infuse a natural passion into the mind, have made it their business to ply the ears, and to stun their Judges by the noise. But Shakespear does not often thus; for the passions in his Scene between Brutus and Cassius are extreamly natural, the thoughts are such as arise from the matter, and the expression of 'em not viciously figurative. I cannot leave this Subject before I do justice to that. Divine Poet, by giving you one of his passionate descriptions: 'tis of Richard the Second when he was depos'd, and led in Triumph through the Streets of London by Henry of Bullingbrook: the painting of it is so lively, and the words so moving, that I have scarce read any thing comparable to it, in any other language, Suppose you have seen already the fortunate Usurper passing through the croud, and follow'd by the shouts and acclamations of the people; and now behold King Richard entring upon the Scene: consider the wretchedness of his condition, and his carriage in it; and refrain from pitty if you can.

> As in a Theatre, the eyes of men
> After a well-grac'd Actor leaves the Stage,
> Are idly bent on him that enters next,
> Thinking his prattle to be tedious:
> Even so, or with much more contempt, mens eyes.
> Did scowl on *Richard*: no man cry'd God save him:
> No joyful tongue gave him his welcom home,
> But dust was thrown upon his Sacred head,
> Which with such gentle sorrow he shook off,
> His face still combating with tears and smiles
> (The badges of his grief and patience)
> That had not God (for some strong purpose) steel'd
> The hearts of men, they must perforce have melted,
> And Barbarism it self have pity'd him.

To speak justly of this whole matter; 'tis neither height of thought that is discommended, nor pathetic vehemence, nor any nobleness of expression in its proper place; but 'tis a false measure of all these, something which is like 'em, and is not them: 'tis the Bristol-stone, which appears like a Diamond; 'tis an extravagant thought, instead of a sublime one; 'tis roaring madness in-
stead

The Preface.

stead of vehemence ; and a sound of words, instead of sence. If Shakespear *were stript of all the Bombast in his passions, and dress'd in the most vulgar words, we should find the beauties of his thoughts remaining ; if his embroideries were burnt down, there would still be silver at the bottom of the melting-pot : but I fear (at least, let me fear it for my self) that we who* Ape *his sounding words, have nothing of his thought, but are all out-side ; there is not so much as a dwarf within our* Giants *cloaths. Therefore, let not* Shakespear *suffer for our sakes ; 'tis our fault, who succeed him in an Age which is more refin'd, if we imitate him so ill, that we coppy his failings only, and make a virtue of that in our Writings, which in his was an imperfection.*

For what remains, the excellency of that Poet was, as I have said, in the more manly passions ; Fletcher's *in the softer :* Shakespear *writ better betwixt man and man ;* Fletcher, *betwixt man and woman : consequently, the one describ'd friendship better ; the other love : yet* Shakespear *taught* Fletcher *to write love ; and* Juliet, *and* Desdemona, *are Originals. 'Tis true, the Scholar had the softer soul ; but the Master had the kinder. Friendship is both a virtue, and a Passion essentially ; love is a passion only in its nature, and is not a virtue but by* Accident : *good nature makes Friendship ; but effeminacy Love.* Shakespear *had an Universal mind, which comprehended all Characters and Passions ;* Fletcher *a more confin'd, and limited : for though he treated love in perfection, yet Honour, Ambition, Revenge, and generally all the stronger Passions, he either touch'd not, or not Masterly. To conclude all ; he was a Limb of* Shakespear.

I had intended to have proceeded to the last property of manners, which is, that they must be constant ; and the characters maintain'd the same from the beginning to the end ; and from thence to have proceeded to the thoughts and expressions sutable to a Tragedy : but I will first see how this will relish with the Age. 'Tis I confess but curs rily written ; yet the Judgment which is given here, is generally founded upon Experience : But because many men are shock'd at the name of Rules, as if they were a kinde of Magisterial prescription upon Poets, I will conclude with the words of Rapin, in his reflections on Aristotles work of Poetry : *If the Rules be well consider'd : we shall find them to be made only to reduce Nature into Method, to trace her step by step, and not to suffer the least mark of her to escape us : 'tis only by these, that probability in Fiction is maintain'd, which is the Soul of Poetry : they are founded upon good Sence, and Sound Reason, rather than on* Authority; *for, though* Aristotle *and* Horace *are produc'd, yet no man must argue, that what they write is true, because they writ it ; but 'tis evident, by the ridiculous mistakes and gross absurdities, which have been made by those Poets who have taken their Fancy only for their guide, that if this Fancy be not regulated, 'tis a meer caprice, and utterly incapable to produce a reasonable and judicious Poem.*

The

The Prologue Spoken by Mr. *Betterton*,
Reprefenting the Ghoft of *Shakefpear*.

SEE, *my lov'd* Britons, *fee your* Shakefpeare *rife*,
An awfull ghoft confefs'd to human eyes!
Unnam'd, methinks, diftinguifh'd I had been
From other fhades, by this eternal green,
About whofe wreaths the vulgar Poets *ftrive,*
And with a touch, their wither'd Bays *revive.*
Untaught, unpractis'd, in a barbarous Age,
I found not, but created firft the Stage.
And, if I drain'd no Greek *or* Latin *ftore,*
'Twas, that my own abundance gave me more.
On foreign trade I needed not rely
Like fruitfull Britain, *rich without fupply.*
In this my rough-drawn Play, you fhall behold
Some Mafter-ftrokes, fo manly and fo bold
That he, who meant to alter, found 'em fuch
He fhook; and thought it Sacrilege to touch.
Now, where are the Succeffours to my name?
What bring they to fill out a Poets fame?
Weak, fhort-liv'd iffues of a feeble Age;
Scarce living to be Chriften'd on the Stage!
For Humour farce, for love they rhyme difpence,
That tolls the knell, for their departed fence.
Dulnefs might thrive in any trade but this:
'T wou'd recommend to fome fat Benefice.
Dulnefs, that in a Playhoufe meets difgrace
Might meet with Reverence, in its proper place.
The fulfome clench that naufeats the Town
Wou'd from a Judge or Alderman go down!
Such virtue is there in a Robe and gown!
And that infipid ftuff which here you hate
Might fomewhere elfe be call'd a grave debate:
Dulnefs is decent in the Church and State.
But I forget that ftill 'tis underftood
Bad Plays are beft decry'd by fhowing good:
Sit filent then, that my pleas'd Soul may fee
A Judging Audience once, and worthy me:
My faithfull Scene from true Records fhall tell
How Trojan *valour did the* Greek *excell;*
Your great forefathers fhall their fame regain,
And Homers *angry Ghoft repine in vain.*

Actors

Persons Reprefented,

By

Hector.	**Mr**. *Smith.*
Troilus.	Mr.*Betterton.*
Priam.	Mr. *Percivall.*
Æneas.	Mr.*Joseph Williams.*
Pandarus.	Mr. *Leigh.*
Calchas.	Mr. *Percivall.*
Agamemnon.	Mr. *Gillo.*
Ulyffes.	Mr. *Harris.*
Achilles.	Mr. *David Williams.*
Ajax.	Mr. *Bright.*
Neftor.	Mr. *Norris.*
Diomedes.	Mr. *Crosby.*
Patroclus.	Mr. *Boman.*
Menelaus.	Mr. *Richards.*
Therfites.	Mr. *Underhill.*
Creffida,	Mrs *Mary Lee.*
Andromache.	Mrs *Betterton.*

Truth

A

TRUTH found too late.

A

TRAGEDY.

ACT I. SCENE I. *A Camp.*

Enter Agamemnon, Menelaus, Ulysses, Diomedes, Nestor.

Agam. PRinces, it seems not strange to us nor new,
That after Nine years Seige *Troy* makes defence,
Since every Action of Recorded Fame
Has with long difficulties been involv'd,
Not Answering that Idea of the thought
Which gave it Birth, why then you Grecian Chiefs,
With sickly Eyes do you behold our labours,
And think 'em our dishonour, which indeed,
Are the protractive Tryals of the Gods,
To prove heroique Constancy in Men?
 Nestor. With due observance of thy Soveraign Seat
Great *Agamemnon*, *Nestor* shall apply,
Thy well-weigh'd words: In struggling with misfortunes,
Lyes the true proof of Virtue: on smooth Seas,
How many bawble Boats dare set their Sails,
And make an equall way with firmer Vessels!
But let the Tempest once inrage that Sea,
And then behold the strong rib'd *Argosie*,
Bounding between the Ocean and the Ayr
Like *Perseus* mounted on his *Pegasus*.
Then where are those weak Rivals of the Maine?
B

Or

Or to avoid the Tempeſt fled to Po᷑ᵗ,
Or made a Prey to *Neptune* : even thus
Do empty ſhow, and true-priz'd worth divide
In ſtorms of Fortune.

    Uliſſes. Mighty *Agamemnon* !
Heart of our Body, Soul of our deſigns,
In whom the tempers, and the minds of all
Shou'd be inclos'd : hear what *Uliſſes* ſpeaks.

    Agam.——You have free leave.

    Uliſſes. Troy had been down ere this, and *Hectors* Sword
Wanted a Maſter but for our diſorders :
The obſervance due to rule has been neglected ;
Obſerve how many *Grecian* Tents ſtand void
Upon this plain ; ſo many hollow factions :
For when the General is not like the Hive
To whom the Foragers ſhould all repair,
What Hony can our empty Combs expect ?
O when Supremacy of Kings is ſhaken,
What can ſucceed : How cou'd communities
Or peacefull traffick from divided ſhores,
Prerogative of Age, Crowns, Scepters, Lawrells,
But by degree ſtand on their ſolid baſe !
Then every thing reſolves to brutal force
And headlong force is led by hoodwink'd will,
For wild Ambition, like a ravenous Woolf,
Spurd on by will and ſeconded by power,
Muſt make an univerſal prey of all,
And laſt devour it ſelf.

    Neſt. Moſt prudently *Uliſſes* has diſcover'd
The Malady whereof our ſtate is ſick.

    Diom. 'Tis truth he ſpeaks, the General's diſdain'd
By him one ſtep beneath, he by the next :
That next by him below : So each degree
Spurns upward at Superiour eminence :
Thus our diſtempers are their ſole ſupport ;
Troy in our weakneſs lives, not in her ſtrength.

    Agam. The Nature of this ſickneſs found, inform us
From whence it draws its birth ?

    Ulyſſes. The great *Achilles* whom opinion crowns
The chief of all our Hoſt——
Having his ears buzz'd with his noiſy Fame
Diſdains thy Sovereign charge, and in his Tent,
Lyes mocking our deſignes, with him *Patroclus*
Upon a lazy Bed, breaks ſcurvil Jeſts
And with ridiculous and awkard action,

                         Which

Which, flanderer, he imitation calls
Mimicks the Grecian chiefs.

    Agam. As how *Ulysses* ?

    Ulysses. Ev'n thee the King of men he do's not spare
(The monkey Authour) but thy greatness Pageants
And makes of it Rehearsals : like a Player
Bellowing his Passion till he break the spring
And his rack'd Voice jar to his Audience ;
So represents he Thee, though more unlike
Then *Vulcan* is to *Venus.*
And at this fulsome stuff, this wit of Apes,
The large *Achilles* on his prest Bed lolling,
From his deep Chest roars out a loud Applause,
Tickling his spleen, and laughing till he wheeze.

    Nestor. Nor are you spar'd *Ulysses,* but as you speak in Council
He hems ere he begins, then strokes his Beard,
Casts down his looks, and winks with half an Eye ;
'Has every action, cadence, motion, tone,
All of you but the sence.

    Agam. Fortune was merry
When he was born, and plaid a trick on Nature
To make a mimick Prince : he ne're acts ill
But when he would seem wise :
For all he says or do's from serious thought
Appears so wretched that he mocks his title
And is his own Buffoon.

    Ulysses. In imitation of this scurril fool
Ajax is grown self-will'd as broad *Achilles,*
He keeps a Table too, makes Factious Feasts,
Rails on our State of War, and sets *Thirsites*
(A slanderous slave of an ore-flowing gall)
To level us with low Comparisons :
    They tax our Policy with Cowardice
Count Wisdom of no moment in the War,
In brief, esteem no Act, but that of hand ;
The still and thoughtful parts which move those hands
With them are but the tasks cut out by fear
To be perform'd by Valour.

    Agam. Let this be granted, and *Achilles* horse
Is more of use then he : but you grave pair
Like time and wisdome marching hand in hand
Must put a stop to these incroaching Ills :
To you we leave the care :
You who con'd show whence the distemper springs
Must vindicate the Dignity of Kings.   *Exeunt.*

B 2   SCENE

SCENE II. *Troy.*

Enter Pandarus, *and* Troilus.

Troil. Why fhould I fight without the Trojan walls
Who, without fighting, am ore'thrown within :
The Trojan who is Mafter of a Soul
Let him to battel, *Troilus* has none.

Pand. Will this never be at an end with you?

Troil. The Greeks are ftrong and skillful to their ftrength
Fierce to their skill, and to their feircenefs wary ;
But I am weaker then a Womans tear ,
Tamer then fleep, fonder then Ignorance :
And Artlefs as unpractic'd Infancy.

Pand. Well, I have told you enough of this ; for my part I'll not
meddle nor make any further in your Love : He that will eat of the
Roaftmeat, muft ftay for the kindling of the fire.

Troil. Have I not ftay'd?

Pand. I, the kindling : but you muft ftay the fpitting of the meat.

Troil. Have I not ftay'd ?

Pand. I, the fpitting : but there's two words to a bargain : you muft
ftay the roafting too.

Troil. Still have I ftay'd : and ftill the farther off.

Pand. That's but the roafting, but there's more in this word ftay ;
there's the taking off the Spitt, the making of the fawce, the difhing,
the fetting on the Table, and the faying Grace ; nay you muft ftay the
cooling too, or you may chance to burn your chaps.

Troil. At *Priams* table penfive do I fit,
And when fair *Creffid* comes into my thoughts
(Can fhe be fay'd to come, who ne're was abfent !)

Pand. Well, fhe's a moft ravifhing creature ; and fhe look'd Yefterday moft killingly, fhe had fuch a ftroke with her eyes, fhe cut to the
quick with every glance of e'm.

Troil. I was about to tell thee, when my heart
Was ready with a figh to cleave in two
Left *Hector*, or my Father fhould perceive me,
I have with mighty anguifh of my Soul
Juft at the Birth ftifled this ftill-born-figh
And forc'd my face into a painful fmile.

Pand. I meafur'd her with my girdle Yefterday; fhe's not half a yard
about the wafte, but fo taper a fhape did I never fee, but when I had
her in my arms , Lord thought I, and by my troth I could not forbear
fighing, if Prince *Troilus* had her at this advantage, and I were holding
of

of the door.——And she were a thought taller, but as she is, she wants not
an Inch of *Hellen* neither ; but there's no more comparison between the
Women——there was wit , there was a sweet tongue : How her
words melteth in her mouth ! *Mercury* wou'd have been glad to have
had such a tongue in his mouth I warrant him.
I wou'd some body had heard her talk Yesterday, as I did :

Troil. Oh *Pandarus*, when I tell thee I am mad
In *Cressid's* Love, thou answer'st she is fair ;
Praisest her eyes, her stature and her wit ;
But praising thus, instead of oyl and balme,
Thou lay'st in every wound her Love has giv'n me
The Sword that made it.

Pand. I give her but her due.

Troil. Thou give'st her not so much.

Pand. Faith 'Ile speak no more of her, let her be as she is :
If she be a beauty 'tis the better for her, and she be not
She has the mends in her own hands for *Pandarus*.

Troil. In spight of me thou wilt mistake my meaning.

Pand. I have had but my labour for my pains,
Ill thought on of her, and ill thought on of you :
Gone between and between, and am ground in the Millstones
For my Labour.

Troil. What art thou angry *Pandarus* with thy friend ?

Pand. Because she's my Niece, therefore she's not so fair as *Hellen*,
and she were not my Niece, show me such another piece of Womans
flesh ; take her limb by limb, I say no more, but if *Paris* had seen her
first, *Menelaus* had been no Cuckold : but what care I if she were a Black-
moore, what am I the better for her face.

Troil. Say'd I she was not beautiful.

Pand. I care not if you did, she's a fool to stay behind her Father
Calchas, let her to the Greeks ; and so I'le tell her : for my part I am
resolute, I'le meddle no more in your affairs.

Troil. But hear me !

Pand. Not I.

Troil. Dear *Pandarus*——

Pand. Pray speak no more on't, I'le not burn my fingers in another body's business, I'le leave it as I found it, & there's an end. [*Exit Pandarus.*

Troil. O Gods, how do you torture me ?
I cannot come to *Cressid* but by him,
And he's as peevish to be woo'd to wooe,
As she is to be won.

Enter Æneas.

Æneas. How now, Prince *Troilus* ; why not in the battle ?

Troil. Because not there, this Womans answer suites me ;

For

For Womannish it is to be from thence :
What news *Æneas* from the field to day ?

   Æn. *Paris* is hurt.

   Troil. By whom ?

   Æn. By *Menelaus.*   Hark what good sport   *Alarum within.*
Is out of Town to day, when I hear such Musick
I cannot hold from dancing.

   Troil. I'le make one,
And try to lose an anxious thought or two
In heat of action.

  [*Aside*] Thus Coward-like from love to War I run,
Seek the less dangers , and the greater shun.   [*Exit* Troil.

Enter Cressida.

   Cressid. My Lord *Æneas,* who were those went by? I mean the Ladys !

   Æn. Queen *Hecuba,* and *Hellen.*

   Cress. And whither go they ?

   Æn. Up to the Western Tower.
Whose height commands as subject, all the vale ;
To see the battle, *Hector* whose patience
Is fix'd like that of Heav'n, to day was mov'd :
He chid *Andromache,* and strook his Armourer,
And as there were good Husbandry in War,
Before the Sun was up he went to field ;
Your pardon Lady that's my business too.   [*Exit* Æneas.

   Cress. *Hectors* a gallant Wariour.

Enter Pandarus.

   Pand. What's that, what's that !

   Cress. Good morrow Uncle *Pandarus.*

   Pand. Good morrow Cousin *Cressida* : when were you at Court ?

   Cress. This morning Uncle !

   Pand. What were you a talking when I came ? was *Hector* arm'd,
And gone ere ye came ? *Hector* was stirring early.

   Cress. That I was talking of; and of his anger !

   Pand. Was he angry say you? true he was so, and I know the cause :
He was struck down yesterday in the battle, but he'll lay about him ;
he'll cry quittance with 'em to day I'le answer for him : and there's
Troilus will not come far behind him ; let 'em take heed of *Troilus,* I
can tell 'em that too.

   Cress. What was he struck down too ?

   Pand. Who, *Troilus* ? *Troilus* is the better man of the two.

   Cress. Oh *Jupiter* ! there's no comparison, *Troilus* the better man !

   Pand. What, no comparison between *Hector* and *Troilus* ? do you
know a man if you see him ?

Cress.

Creſſi. No, for he may look like a man, and not be one.

Pand. Well, I ſay *Troilus* is *Troilus*.

Creſſi. That's what I ſay, for I am ſure he is not *Hector*.

Pand. No, nor *Hector* is not *Troilus*, make your beſt of that Neece!

Creſſi. 'Tis true, for each of 'em is himſelf.

Pand. Himſelf! alas poor *Troilus* ! I wou'd he were himſelf, well the Gods are allſufficient, and time muſt mend or end : I wou'd he were himſelf, and wou'd I were a Lady for his ſake. I would not anſwer for my Maidenhead,——No, *Hector* is not a better man than *Troilus*.

Creſſi. Excuſe me.

Pand. Pardon me : *Troilus* is in the bud ; 'tis early day with him, you ſhall tell me another tale when *Troilus* is come to bearing : and yet he'll not bear neither in ſome ſence. No, *Hector* ſhall never have his virtues.

Creſſi. No matter.

Pand. Nor his beauty, nor his faſhion, nor his wit, he ſhall have nothing of him.

Creſſi. They would not become him, his own are better.

Pand. How, his own better ! you have no judgment Neece, *Hellen* her ſelf ſwore tother day, that *Troilus* for a manly brown complexion ; (for ſo it is, I muſt confeſs ;) not brown neither.

Creſſi. No, but very brown.

Phnd. Faith to ſay truth, brown and not brown : come I ſwear to you, I think *Hellen* loves him better then *Paris* : Nay I'm ſure ſhe does, ſhe comes me to him tother day, into the bow window, and you know *Troilus* has not above three or four hairs on his chin.

Creſſi. That's but a bare commendation.

Pand. But to prove to you that *Hellen* loves him, ſhe comes, and puts me her white hand to his cloven chin !

Creſſi. Has he been fighting then, how came it cloven ?

Pand. Why, you know it is dimpled. I cannot chooſe but laugh to think how ſhe tickled his cloven chin : She has a marvellous white hand I muſt needs confeſs.
But let that paſs, for I know who has a whiter :
Well Couſin I told you a thing yeſterday, think on't, think on't.

Creſſi. So I do Uncle.

Pand. I'le beſworn 'tis true ; he will weep ye, and 'twere a man born in *April*.   [*A Retreat ſounded.*
Hark, they are returning from the field ; ſhall we ſtay and ſee 'em as they come by, ſweet Neece do, ſweet Neece *Creſſida.*

Creſſi. For once you ſhall command me.

Pand. Here, here, here's an excellent place ; we may ſee 'em here moſt bravely, and I'le tell you all their names as they paſs by : but mark *Troilus* above the reſt, mark *Troilus*, he's worth your marking.

                                                        Æneas

Æneas paffes over the Stage.

Creff. Speak not fo loud then.

Pand. That's *Æneas*, Is't not a brave man that, he's a fwinger, many a *Grecian* he has laid with his face upward ; but mark *Troilus*, you fhall fee anon.

Enter Anthenor, *paffing.*

That's *Anthenor*, he has a notable head-peece I can tell you, and he's the ableft man for judgment in all *Troy*, you may turn him loofe i'faith, and by my troth a proper perfon : When comes *Troilus* ? I'le fhow you *Troilus* anon, if he fee me, you fhall fee him nod at me.

Hector paffes over.

That's *Hector*, that, that, look you that, there's a fellow, go thy way *Hector*, there's a brave man Neece : O brave *Hector*, look how he looks ! there's a countenance ! is't not a brave man Neece ?

Creff. I always told you fo.

Pand. Is a not ? it does a mans heart good to look on him, look you, look you there, what hacks are on his Helmet : this was no boys play i'faith, he laid it on with a vengeance, take it off whofe who's will as they fay ! there are hacks Neece !

Creff. Were thofe with Swords.

Pand. Swords, or Bucklers, Faulchions, Darts, and Lances ! any thing he cares not ! and the devil come 'tis all one to him, by *Jupiter* he looks fo terribly that I am half afraid to praife him.

Enter Paris.

Yonder comes *Paris*, yonder comes *Paris*, look ye yonder Neece ; is't not a brave young Prince too ! He draws the beft bow in all *Troy*, he hits you to a fpan twelvefcore level ; who faid he came home hurt to day : why this will do *Hellen's* heart good now ! Ha ! that I cou'd fee *Troilus* now !

Enter Helenus.

Creff. Who's that black man Uncle ?

Pand. That's *Helenus*, I marvel where *Troilus* is all this while? that's *Helenus*, I think *Troilus* went not forth to day ; that's *Helenus*.

Creff. Can *Helenus* fight Uncle ?

Pand. *Helenus* ! No, yes, he'll fight indifferently well, I marvel in my heart what's become of *Troilus*? Hark ! do you not hear the people cry *Troilus* ? *Helenus* is a Prieft and keeps a whore ; he'll fight for's whore, or he's no true Prieft I warrant him.

Enter Troilus *paffing over.*

Creff. What fneaking fellow comes yonder ?

Pand.

Pand. Where, yonder! that's *Deiphobus*: No I lye, I lye, that's *Troilus*, there's a man Neece *!* hem! O brave *Troilus*! the Prince of chivalry, and flower of fidelity!

Cressi. Peace, for shame peace.

Pand. Nay but mark him then,*!* O brave *Troilus*! there's a man of men Neece *!* look you how his Sword is bloody, and his Helmet more hack'd then *Hectors*, and how he looks, and how he goes! O admirable youth! he nere saw two and twenty. Go thy way *Troilus*, go thy way *!* had I a sister were a grace, and a daughter a Goddesse, he shou'd take his choice of 'em, O admirable man! *Paris! Paris* is dirt to him, and I warrant *Hellen* to change, wou'd give all the shooes in her shop to boot.

Enter Common Souldiers passing over.

Cressi. Here come more.

Pand. Asses, fools, dolts, dirt and dung, stuff and lumber *:* porredg after meat? but I cou'd live and dye with *Troilus*. Nere look Neece, nere look, the Lyons are gone ; Apes and Monkeys, the fag end of the creation. I had rather be such a man as *Troilus*, then *Agamemnon* and all *Greece.*

Cressi. There's *Achilles* among the Greeks, he's a brave man!

Pand. *Achilles*! a Carman, a beast of burden ; a very Camel, have you any eyes Neece, do you know a man *!* is he to be compar'd with *Troilus* *!*

Enter Page.

Page. Sir, my Lord *Troilus* wou'd instantly speak with you.

Pand. Where boy, where!

Page. At his own house, if you think convenient.

Pand. Good boy tell him I come instantly, I doubt he's wounded, farewell good Neece : But I'le be with you by and by.

Cressi. To bring me Uncle!

Pand. I, a token from Prince *Troilus.*

Cressi. By the same token you are a procurer Uncle. [*Exit* Pandarus.

Cressida *alone.*

A strange dissembling Sex we Women are,
Well may we men, when we our selves deceive.
Long has my secret Soul lov'd *Troilus.*
I drunk his praises from my Uncles mouth,
As if my ears cou'd nere be satisfi'd ;
Why then, why said I not, I love this Prince?
How cou'd my tongue conspire against my heart,
To say I lov'd him not, O childish love !
'Tis like an Infant froward in his play,
And what he most desires, he throws away.   [*Exit* Cressida.

C

ACT.

ACT II. SCENE I. *Troy.*

Priam, Hector, Troilus, Æneas.

Priam. AFter th' expence of so much time and blood,
Thus once again the Grecians send to *Troy.*
Deliver *Hellen,* and all other loss
Shall be forgotten *Hector,* what say you to't?

Hect. Though no man less can fear the Greeks than I,
Yet there's no Virgin of more tender heart
More ready to cry out, who knows the consequence,
Then *Hector* is; for modest doubt is mix'd
With manly courage best; let *Hellen* go.
If we have lost so many lives of ours,
To keep a thing not ours; not worth to us
The vallue of a man, what reason is there
Still to retain the cause of so much ill?

Troil. Fy, fy, my noble Brother!
Weigh you the worth and honour of a King,
So great as *Asia's* Monarch in a scale
Of common ounces thus?
Are fears and reasons fit to be consider'd,
When a Kings fame is question'd?

Hect. Brother, she's not worth
What her defence has cost us.

Troil. What's ought but as 'tis vallued?

Hect. But vallue dwels not in opinion only:
It holds the dignity and estimation,
As well, wherein 'tis precious of it self.
As in the prizer, 'tis Idolatry
To make the Service greater than the God.

Troil. We turn not back the Silks upon the Merchant
When we have worn 'em: the remaining food
Throw not away because we now are full.
If you confess 'twas wisedome *Paris* went,
As you must needs; for you all cry'd go, go,
If you'll confess he brought home noble prize
As you must needs, for you all clapt your hands,
And cry'd inestimable: why do you now
So underrate the vallue of your purchase?
For let me tell you 'tis unmanly theft
When we have taken what we fear to keep!

Æne. There's not the meanest Spirit in our party

Without

Without a heart to dare, or Sword to draw,
When *Hellen* is defended : none so noble
Whose life were ill bestowed, or death unfam'd,
When *Hellen* is the Subject.

    Priam. So says *Paris.*
Like one besotted on effeminate joys,
He has the honey still, but these the gall.

    Æneas. He not proposes meerly to himself
The pleasures such a beauty brings with it:
But he wou'd have the stain of *Hellen's* rape
Wip'd off in honourable keeping her.

    Hect. Troilus and *Æneas* you have sayd :
If saying superficiall things be reason.
But if this *Hellen* be anothers wife,
The Morall laws of Nature and of Nation's
Speak loud she be restor'd : thus to persist
In doing wrong, extenuates not wrong,
But makes it much more so : *Hectors* opinion
Is this, is in way of truth : yet ne'retheless
My sprightly Brother I encline to you
In resolution to defend her still :
For 'tis a cause on which our *Trojan* honour
And common reputation will depend.

    Troil. Why there you touch'd the life of our designe :
Were it not glory that we covet more
Then war and vengeance (beasts and womens pleasure)
I wou d not wish a drop of *Trojan* blood
Spent more in her defence : But oh my Brother
She is a subject of renoun and honour,
And I presume brave *Hector* wou'd not lose
The rich advantage of his future fame
For the wide worlds revenew : ——I have businefs ;
But glad I am to leave you thus resolv'd.
When such arms strike, ne're doubt of the success.

    Æneas. May we not guesse ?
    Troil. You may, and be deceiv'd.   [*Exit* Troil.
    Hect. A woman on my life : ev'n so it happens,
Religion, state affairs, whater'es the theme
It ends in women still.

Enter Andromache.

    Priam. See here's your wife
To make that maxim good.
    Hect. Welcome *Andromache* : your looks are cheerfull ;
You bring some pleasing news.

                             Andro.

Andro. Nothing that's ferious.
Your little Son *Aftyanax* has employ'd me
As his Ambaffadreffe.

Hect. Upon what errand?

Andro. No lefs then that his Grandfather this day
Would make him Knight : he longs to kill a *Grecian* :
For fhou'd he ftay to be a man, he thinks
Youll kill 'em all ; and leave no work for him.

Priam. Your own blood, *Hector.*

Andro. And therefore he defignes to fend a challenge
To *Agamemnon, Ajax,* or *Achilles*
To prove they do not well to burn our fields;
And keep us coop'd like prifner's in a Town :
To lead this lazy life.

Hect. What fparks of honour
Fly from this child ! the God's fpeak in him fure :
——It fhall be fo——I'le do't.

Priam. What means my Son?

Hect. To fend a challenge to the boldeft *Greek*;
Is not that Country ours? thofe fruitfull Fields
Wafh'd by yon Silver flood, are they not ours?
Thofe teeming Vines that tempt our longing eyes,
Shall we behold e'm? fhall we call e'm ours
And dare not make e'm fo? by Heavens I'le know
Which of thefe haughty *Grecians,* dares to think
He can keep *Hector* prifner here in *Troy.*

Priam. If *Hector* only were a private Man,
This wou'd be courage, but in him 'tis madnefs.
The generall fafety on your life depends ;
And fhcu'd you perifh in this rafh attempt
Troy with a groan, would feel her Soul go out:
And breath her laft in you.

Æneas. The task you uudertake is hazardous :
Suppofe you win, what wou'd the profit be?
If *Ajax* or *Achilles* fell beneath
Your thundring Arm, wou'd all the reft depart?
Wou'd *Agamemnon,* or his injur'd Brother
Set fayl for this? then it were worth your danger :
But, as it is, we throw our utmoft ftake
Againft whole heaps of theirs.

Priam. He tells you true.

Æneas. Suppofe one, *Ajax,* or *Achilles* loft.
They can repair with more that fingle lofs :
Troy has but one, one *Hector.*

Hect. No *Æneas?*

What

What then art thou; and what is *Troilus*?
What will *Aftyanax* be?
   Priam. An *Hector* one day.
But you muft let him live to be a *Hector*.
And who fhall make him fuch when you are gone?
Who fhall inftrnct his tendernefs in arms,
Or give his childhood leffons of the war?
Who fhall defend the promife of his youth
And make it bear in Manhood? the young Sappling
Is fhrowded long beneath the Mother tree
Before it be tranfplanted from its Earth,
And truft it felf for growth.
   Hect. Alas, my Father!
You have not drawn one reafon from your felf,
But publick fafety, and my Sons green years :
In this neglecting that main argument
Truft me you chide my filiall piety :
As if I cou'd be won from my refolves
By *Troy*, or by my Son, or any name
More dear to me than yours.
   Priam. I did not name my felf; becaufe I know
When thou art gone, I need no *Grecian* Sword,
To help me dye, but only *Hectors* lofs.
Daughter, why fpeak not you? why ftand you filent?
Have you no right in *Hector*, as a wife?
   Andro. I would be worthy to be *Hectors* wife :
And had I been a Man, as my Soul's one
I had afpir'd a nobler name, his friend.
How I love *Hector*, (need I fay I love him?)
I am not but in him :
But when I fee him arming for his Honour,
His Country and his Gods, that martial fire
That mounts his courage, kindles ev'n to me :
And when the Trojan Matrons wait him out
With pray'rs, and meet with bleffings his return ;
The pride of Virtue, beats within my breaft,
To wipe away the fweat and duft of War :
And drefs my Heroe, glorious in his wounds.
   Hect. Come to my Arms, thou manlier Virtue come;
Thou better Name than wife! wou'dft thou not blufh   [*Embrace.*
To hug a coward thus?
   Priam. Yet ftill I fear !
   Andro. There fpoke a woman, pardon Royal Sir ;
Has he not met a thoufand lifted Swords,
Of thick rank'd *Grecians*, and fhall one affright him?

There's not a day but he encounters Armies;
And yet as safe, as if the broad brim'd Shield
That *Pallas* wears, were held 'twixt him and death.

   Hect. Thou knowst me well; and thou shalt praise me more,
Gods make me worthy of thee!

   Andro. You shall be
My Knight this day, you shall not wear a cause
So black as *Hellens* rape upon your breast,
Let *Paris* fight for *Hellen*; guilt for guilt,
But when you fight for Honour and for me,
Then let our equal Gods behold an Act,
They may not blush to Crown.

   Hect. Æneas go.
And bear my Challenge to the Grecian Camp,
If there be one amongst the best of *Greece*,
Who holds his honour higher then his ease,
Who knows his valour, and knows not his fear;
Who loves his Mistress more then in confession:
And dares avow her beauty and her worth,
In other Arms then hers; to him this Challenge.
I have a Lady of more truth and beauty,
Then ever *Greek* did compass in his arms:
And will to morrow, with the Trumpets call,
Mid-way, between their Tents, and these our Walls,
Maintains what I have said, if any come
My Sword shall honour him, if none shall dare,
Then shall I say at my return to *Troy*,
The Grecian dames, are Sun-burnt, and not worth
The splinter of a Lance.

   Æneas. It shall be told 'em,
As boldly as you gave it.

   Priam. Heav'n protect thee.

                               [*Exeunt Omnies.*

SCENE II.

Pandarus, Cressid.

   Pand. YOnder he stands poor wretch! there stands he, with such a look, and such a face, and such begging eyes; there he stands poor prisoner.

   Cress. What a deluge of words do you pour out Uncle, to say just nothing?

Pand.

Pand. Nothing do you call it, is that nothing, do you call it nothing? why he looks for all the World, like one of your rascally Malefactors, just thrown off the Gibbet, with his cap down, his arms ty'd down, his feet sprunting, his body swinging, nothing do you call it? this is nothing with a vengeance.

Cressi. Or, what think you of a hurt bird, that flutters about with a broken wing?

Pand. Why go to then, he cannot fly away then, then, that's certain, that's undoubted: there he lies to be taken up: but if you had seen him, when I said to him, take a good heart man, and follow me: and fear no colours, and speak your mind man: she can never stand you: she will fall, and 'twere a leaf in Autumn.

Cress. Did you tell him all this without my consent?

Pand. Why you did consent, your eyes consented; they blab'd, they leer'd, their very corners blabb'd. But you'll say your tongue sayd nothing. No I warrant it: your tongue was wiser; your tongue was better bred: your tongue kept its own counsell: Nay, 'le say that for you, your tongue sayd nothing. Well such a shamefac'd couple did I never see days o' my life: so fraid of one another; such ado to bring you to the business: well if this job were well over, if ever I lose my pains again with an awkard couple, let me be painted in the signe-post for the *Labour in vain*: fye upon't, fye upon't; there's no conscience in't: all honest people will cry shame on't.

Cress. Where is this Monster to be shown? what's to be given for a sight of him?

Pand Why ready money, ready money; you carry it about you: give and take is square-dealing; for in my conscience he's as errant a maid as you are: I was fain to use violence to him, to pull him hither: and he pull'd and I pull'd: for you must know he's absolutely the strongest youth in *Troy*: to'ther day he took *Hellen* in one hand, and *Paris* in to'ther, and danc'd 'em at one another at arms-end, and 'twere two Moppets: there was a back, there were bone and Sinnews: there was a back for you.

Cressi. For these good procuring Offices you'l be damn'd one day Uncle.

Pand. Who I damn'd? faith I doubt I shall: by my troth I think I shall, nay if a man be damn'd for doing good, as thou saist, it may go hard with me.

Cressi. Then I'le not see Prince *Troilus*, I'le not be accessary to your damnation.

Pand. How, not see Prince *Troilus*? why I have engag'd, I have promis'd, I have past my word, I care not for damning, let me alone for damning; I vallue not damning in comparison with my word. If I am damn'd it shall be a good damning to thee girl, thou shalt be my

heir,

heir, come 'tis a virtuous girl, thou fhalt help me to keep my word, thou fhalt fee Prince *Troilus.*

Creffi. The ventures great.

Pand. No venture in the World, thy Mother ventur'd it for thee, and thou fhalt venture it for my little Coufin that muft be.

Creffi. Weigh but my fears, Prince *Troilus* is young.——

Pand. Marry is he, there's no fear in that I hope, the fear were if he were old and feeble.

Creffi. And I a woman.

Pand. No fear yet, thou art a Woman, and he's a Man, put them two together, put 'em together.

Creffi. And if I fhou'd be frail.——

Pand. There's all my fear that thou art not frail : thou fhou'dft be frail, all flefh is frail.

Creffi. Are you my Uncle, and can give this counfel to your own Brothers daughter.

Pand. If thou wert my own daughter a thoufand times over, I cou'd do no better for thee, what wou'dft thou have girl, he's a Prince and a young Prince, and a loving young Prince ! an Uncle doft thou call me, by *Cupid* I am a father to thee; get thee in, get thee in girl, I hear him coming. And do you hear Neice ! I give you leave,

[*Exit Creffida.*

to deny a little 'twill be decent : but take heed of obftinacy, that's a vice; no obftinacy my dear Niece.

Enter Troylus.

Troil. Now *Pandarus.*

Pand. Now, my fweet Prince ! have you feen my Niece ? no I know you have not.

Troylus; No *Pandarus*; I ftalk about your doors
Like a ftrange Soul upon the ftygian banks
Staying for waftage : O be thou my *Charon,*
And give me a fwift tranfportanee to *Elyfium,*
And fly with me to *Creffida.*

Pand. Walk here a moment more : I'le bring her ftraight.

Troil. I fear fhe will not come : moft fure fhe will not.

Pand. How not come, and I her Uncle ! why I tell you Prince, fhe twitters at you. Ah poor fweet Rogue, ah little Rogue, now does fhe think, and think, and think again of what muft be betwixt you two. Oh fweet,—oh fweet—O——what not come, and I her Uncle ?

Troil. Still thou flatter'ft me ; but prithee flatter ftill ; for I wou'd hope ; I wou'd not wake out of my pleafing dream : oh hope how fweet thou art ! but to hope always, and have no effect of what we hope !

Pand. Oh faint heart, faint heart ! well there's much good matter in thefe old proverbs! No, fhe'll not come I warrant her; fhe has no
bloud

blood of mine in her, not so much as will fill a flea: but if she does not come, and come, and come with a swing into your arms, I say no more, but she has renounc'd all grace, and there's an end.

Troil. I will believe thee: go then, but be sure:

Pand. No, you wou'd not have me go; you are indifferent: shall I go say you: speak the word then:——yet I care not: you may stand in your own light; and lose a sweet young Ladies heart: well, I shall not go then!

Troil. Fly, fly, thou tortur'st me.

Pand. Do I so, do i so! do I torture you indeed! well I will go.

Troil. But yet thou dost not go?

Pand. I go immediately, directly, in a twinkling, with a thought. yet you think a man never does enough for you: I have been labouring in your business like any Moyle. I was with Prince *Paris* this morning, to make your excuse at night for not supping at Court: and I found him, faith how do you think I found him; it does my heart good to think how I found him: yet you think a man never does enough for you.

Troil. Will you go then, what's this to *Cressida?*

Pand. Why you will not hear a Man; what's this to *Cressida?* why I found him abed, abed with *Hellena* by my troth: 'tis a sweet Queen, a sweet Queen, a very sweet Queen;——but she's nothing to my Cousin *Cressida*; she's a blowse, a gipsie, a Tawney-moor to my Cousin *Cressida*: And she lay with one white arm underneath the whorsons neck: oh such a white, lilly white, round, plump arm it was——and you must know it was stript up to th'elbows: and she did so kisse him, and so huggle him:——as who shou'd say——

Troil. But still thou stay'st: what's this to *Cressida?*

Pand. Why I made your excuse to your Brother *Paris*; that I think's to *Cressida*; but such an arm, such a hand, such taper fingers, tother hand was under the bed-cloaths, that I saw not, I confess, that hand I saw not.

Troil. Again thou tortur'st me.

Pand. Nay I was tortur'd too; old as I am, I was tortur'd too: but for all that, I cou'd make a shift, to make him, to make your excuse, to make your father;——by *Jove* when I think of that hand, I am so ravish'd, that I know not what I say: I was tortur'd too.

[Troilus *turns away discontented.*

Well I go, I go; I fetch her, I bring her, I conduct her: not come quoth a, and I her Uncle! *Exit Pandarus.*

Troilus. Im'e giddy; expectation whirls me round:
The imaginary relish is so sweet,
That it enchants my sence; what will it be
When I shall taste that Nectar?
It must be either death, or joy too fine

D   For

For the capacity of human powers.
I fear it much : and I do fear befide,
That I fhall lofe diftinction in my joys :
As does a battle, when they charge on heaps
A flying Enemy.

Re-enter Pandarus.

Pand. She's making her ready : fhe'll come ftraight, you muft be witty now ; fhe does fo blufh, and fetches her breath fo fhort, as if fhe were frighted with a fpright : 'tis the prettieft villain, fhe fetches her breath fo fhort, as 'twere a new ta'ne Sparrow.

Troil. Juft fuch a paffion, does heave up my breaft!
My heart beats thicker than a feavourifh pulfe :
I know not where I am, nor what I do :
Juft like a flave, at unawares encountring
The eye of Majefty :——Leade on, I'le follow.

Exeunt together.

SCENE III. *The Camp.*

Neftor, Ulyffes.

Ulyff. I have conceiv'd an embryo in my brain :
Be you my time to bring it to fome fhape.
Neft. What is't, *Ulyffes?*
Ulyff. The feeded pride,
That has to this maturity blown up
In rank *Achilles,* muft or now be cropt,
Or fhedding, breed a nurfery of like ill,
To overtop us all.
Neft. That's my opinion.
Uliff. This challenge which *Æneas* brings from *Hector,*
However it be fpred in general terms,
Relates in purpofe only to *Achilles.*
And will it wake him to the anfwer think you?
Neft. It ought to do : whom can we elfe oppofe
Who cou'd from *Hector* bring his honour off,
If not *Achilles?* the Succeffe of this
Although particular, will give an Omen
Of good or bad, ev'n to the general caufe.
Ulyff. Pardon me *Neftor,* if I contradict you.
Therefore 'tis fit *Achilles* meet not *Hector.*
Let us like Merchants fhow our courfeft wares,
And think perchance they'll fell : but if they do not,
The luftre of our better yet unfhown
Will fhow the better ; let us not confent

Our

Our greateſt warriour ſhou'd be match'd with *Hector*.
For both our honour and our ſhame in this,
Shall be attended with ſtrange followers.

   Neſt. I ſee e'm not with my old eyes; what are they?
   Ulyſs. What glory our *Achilles* gains from *Hector*.
Were he not proud we all ſhould ſhare with him:
But he already is too inſolent:
And we had better parch in *Affrick* Sun
Than in his pride, ſhou'd he ſcape *Hector* fair.
But grant he ſhou'd be foyl'd
Why then our common reputation ſuffers,
In that of our beſt Man: No, make a Lottery;
And by device let blockiſh *Ajax* draw
The chance to fight with *Hector*: among our ſelves
Give him allowance as the braver Man;
For that will phyſick the great Myrmidon,
Who ſwells with loud applauſe; and make him fall
His Creſt, if brainleſs *Ajax* come ſafe off.
If not, we yet preſerve a fair opinion,
That we have better men.

   Neſt. Now I begin to reliſh thy advice:
Come let us go to *Agamemnon* ſtraight,
T'inform him of our project.

   Ulyſs. 'Tis not ripe.
The skilfull Surgeon will not lanch a ſore
Till Nature has digeſted and prepar'd
The growing humours to his healing purpoſe.
Elſe muſt he often grieve the patients ſence,
When one inciſion once well-time'd wou'd ſerve:
Are not *Achilles*, and dull *Ajax* friends?

   Neſt. As much as fools can be.
   Ulyſs. That knot of friendſhip firſt muſt be unty'd
Ere we can reach our ends; for while they love each other
Both hating us, will draw too ſtrong a byaſſe,
And all the Camp will lean that way they draw:
For brutall courage is the Soldiers Idoll:
So, if one prove contemptuous, back'd by to ther,
'Twill give the law to cool and ſober ſence,
And place the power of war in Mad-mens hands.

   Neſt. Now I conceive you; were they once divided,
And one of them made ours, that one would check
The others towring growth: and keep both low,
As Inſtruments, and not as Lords of war.
And this muſt be by ſecret coals of envy,
Blown in their breſt: compariſons of worth;

                                            Great

Great actions weigh'd of each : and each the beft,
As we fhall give him voice.
  Ulyff. Here comes *Therfites.*

Enter Therfites.

Who feeds on *Ajax* : yet loves him not, becaufe he cannot love.
But as a *Species,* differing from mankinde,
Hatss all he fees; and rails at all he knows;
But hates them moft, from whom he moft receives.
Difdaining that his lot fhou'd be fo low.
That he fhou'd want the kindenefs which he takes.
  Neft. There's none fo fit an Engine : Save ye. *Therfites.*
  Ulyff. Hayl noble *Grecian,* Thou relief of toyls,
Soul of our mirth, and joy of fullen war.
In whofe converfe our winter-nights are fhort,
And Summer-days not tedious.
  Therf. Hang you both.
  Neft. How hang us both!
  Therf. But hang thee firft, thou very reverend fool!
Thou faplefs Oke, that liv'ft by wanting thought.
And now in thy three hundreth year repin'ft
Thou fhould'ft be fell'd : hanging's a civil death,
The death of men : thou canft not hang : thy trunk.
Is only fit for gallows to hang others.
  Neft. A fine greeting.
  Therf. A fine old Dotard, to repine at hanging
At fuch an Age! what faw the Gods in thee
That a Cock- Sparrow fhou'd but live three years,
And thou fhoud'ft laft three Ages! he's thy better;
He ufes life: he treads himfelf to death.
Thou haft forgot thy ufe fome hdndred years :
Thou ftump of Man, thou worn-out broom : thou lumber.
  Neft. I'le hear no more of him, his poyfon works;
What curfe me for my age!
  Ulyff. Hold, you miftake him, *Neftor*; 'tis his cuftome:
What malice is there in a mirthfull fcene!
'Tis but a keen-edg'd Sword, fpread o're with balme
To heal the wound it makes :.
  Therf. Thou beg'ft a curfe!
May'ft thou quit fcores then, and be hang'd on *Neftor,*
Who hangs on thee: thou lead'ft him by the nofe :
Thou play'ft him like a puppet; fpeak'ft within him,
And when thou haft contriv'd fome dark defign
To loofe a thoufand *Greeks*; make dogs meat of us,
Thou layft thy Cuckows egg within his neft,

And

And mak'ſt him hatch it: teacheſt his remembrance
To lye; and ſay, the like of it was practis'd
Two hundred years ago; thou bring'ſt the brain
And he brings only beard to vouch thy plots;
   Neſt I'me no mans fool.
   Therſ. Then be thy own, that's worſe.
   Neſt. He'll rail all day.
   Ulyſs. Then we ſhall learn all day.
Who forms the body to a gracefull carriage
Muſt imitate our awkard motions firſt;
The ſame preſcription does the wiſe *Therſites*
Apply to mend our minds. The ſame he uſes
To *Ajax*, to *Achilles*; to the reſt;
His Satyrs are the phyſick of the Camp.
   Therſ. Wou'd they were poyſon to't, Rats-bane and Hemlock:
Nothing elſe can mend you; and thoſe two brawny fools.
   Ulyſs. He hits e'm right:
Are they not ſuch my *Neſtor*?
   Thers. Dolt-heads, Aſſes.
And beaſts of burtheu; *Ajax* and *Achilles*!
The pillars, no, the porters of the war.
Hard-headed Rogues! Engines, meer wooden Engines,
Puſh'd on to do your work.
   Neſt. They are indeed.
   Therſ. But what a Rogue art thou
To ſay they are indeed: Heaven made e,m horſes
And thou put'ſt on their harneſſe: rid'ſt and ſpur'ſt e'm:
Uſurp'ſt upon heav'ns fools, and mak'ſt e'm thine.
   Neſt. No: they are headſtrong fools to be corrected
By none but by *Therſites*: thou alone
Canſt tame, and train e'm to their proper uſe;
And doing this mayſt claim a juſt reward
From *Greece*, and Royall *Agamemnons* hands.
   Therſ. Ay, when you need a man, you talk of giving;
For wit's a dear commodity among you:
But when you do not want him, then ſtale porridge,
A ſtarv'd dog wou'd not lap; and furrow water
Is all the wine we taſte, give drabs and pimps:
He have no gifts with hooks at end of e'm.
   Ulyſs. Is this a Man, O *Neſtor* to be bought!
Aſia's not price enough! bid the world for him.
And ſhall this man, this *Hermes* this *Apollo*,
Sit lagg of *Ajax* table? almoſt minſtrell,
And with his preſence grace a brainleſs feaſt?
Why they con ſence from him grow wits by rote,

                                  And

And yet, by ill repeating, libell him;
Making his wit their nonfence: nay they fcorn him;
Call him bought rayler, mercenary tongue!
Play him for fport at meals, and kick him off.

   Thers. Yes they can kick, my buttocks feel they can:
They have their Affes tricks: but I'le eat pebbles,
Ile ftarve; 'tis brave to ftarve, 'tis like a Soldier;
Before I'le feed thofe wit-ftarv'd rogues with fence.
They fhall eat dry, and choke for want of wit,
Ere they be moiften'd with one drop of mine.
Ajax, and *Achilles*, two mudd-walls of fool,
That only differ in degrees of thickneffe.

   Ulyf. I'de be reveng'd of both, when wine fumes high,
Set e'm to prate, to boaft their brutall ftrength,
To vye their ftupid courage, till they quarrell
And play at hard-head with their empty Skulls.

   Thers. Yes; they fhall but and kick; and all the while
Ile think they kick for me: they fhall fell timber
On both fides; and then log-wood will be cheap.

   Neft. And *Agamemnon*——

   Thers. Pox of *Agamemnon*;
Cannot I do a mifchief for my felf
But he muft thank me for't!

                    Ulyf. to *Neftor.*
Away; our work is done.   *Exeunt Ulyffes, Neftor.*

   Thers. This *Agamemnon* is a King of clouts:
A chip in porredge.

                 Enter Ajax.

   Ajax. *Therfites!*

   Thers. Set up to frighten Daws from Cherry trees.

   Ajax. Dogg!

   Thers. A ftandard to march under!

   Ajax Thou bitch-woolf! canft thou not hear! feel then.
                                 Strikes him.

   Thers. The plague of *Greece*, and *Hellens* Pox light on thee,
Thou mungrill maftiffe; thou beef-witted Lord.

   Ajax. Speak then, thou mouldy leaven of the Camp.
Speak or Ile beat thee into handfomenefs.

   Thirs. I fhall fooner rayle thee into wit: thou canft kick, canft thou?
A red murrayn on thy Jades tricks!

   Ajax. Tell me the Proclamation:

   Thers. Thou art proclaim'd a fool I think.

   Ajax. You whorfon Cur take that.   [*Strikes him.*

   Thers. Thou Scurvy valiant Affe.

   Ajax. Thou flave.

                                 Therf.

Thers. Thou Lord! ——I, do, do,——wou'd my buttocks were Iron for thy fake.

Enter Achilles. Patroclus.

Achill. Why how now *Ajax* ! wherefore do you this ?
How now *Therfites*, what's the matter man *!*

Thers. I fay this *Ajax* wears his wit in's belly, and his guts in brains.

Achill. Peace fool.

Thers. I wou'd have peace ; but the fool will not.

Prtrocl. But what's the quarrell !

Ajax. I bad him tell me the proclamation, and he rails upon me.

Thers. I ferve thee not :

Ajax. I fhall cut out your tongue !

Thers.'Tis no matter; I fhall fpeak as much fence as thou afterwards : Ile fee you hang'd ere I come any more to your Tent: Ile keep where theres wit ftirring, and leave the faction of fools.—— [*going.*

Achill. Nay, thou fhalt not go *Therfites*, till we have fquees'd the venome out of thee : prithee inform us of this Proclamation.

Thers. Why you empty fuz-balls, your heads are full of nothing elfe but Proclamations.

Ajax. Tell us the news I fay.

Thirs. You fay ! why you never faid any thing in all your life !
But fince you will know, 'tis proclam'd through the Army, that *Hector* is to cudgeil you to morrow.

Achilles. How cudgell him, *Therfites* !

Thers. Nay, you may take a childs part ont if you have fo much courage, for *Hector* has challeng'd the toughest of the *Greeks* : and 'tis in difpute which of your two heads is the fonndest timber.
A knotty piece of work he'll have betwixt your noddles,

Achill. If *Hector* be to fight with any *Greeke*,
He knows his Man.

Ajax. Yes ; he may know his man, without Art *Magick*.

Thers. So he had need : for to my certain knowledge neither of you two are conjurers to inform him.

Achill. to *Ajax.* You do not mean your felf, fure.

Ajax. I mean nothing

Thers. Thou mean'ft fo always.

Achill. Uhh ! mean nothing !

Thers, afide. *Jove* if it be thy will, let thefe two fools quarrell about nothing : 'tis a caufe that's worthy of 'em.

Ajax. You fayd he knew his Man: is there but one ?
One Man amongft the *Greeks* !

Achill. Since you will have it, but one to fight with *Hector*.

Ajax. Then I am he ;

Achil.

Achill. Weak *Ajax.*

Ajax. Weak *Achilles.*

Thers. Weak indeed : God help you both !

Patroc. Come, this muſt be no quarrell.

Thers, There's no cauſe for't.

Patroc. He tells you true ; you are both equall

Thers. Fools.

Achill. I can brook no compariſons.

Ajax. Nor I.

Achill. Well *Ajax.*

Ajax. Well *Achilles.*

Thers. So now they quarrell in *Monoſyllables* : A word and a blow, and't be thy will.

Achill. You may hear more.

Ajax. I wou'd.

Achill. Expect,

Ajax. Farewell.   *Exeunt ſeverally.*

Therſ. Curſe on them, they want wine ; your trne fool will never fight without it. Or a drab a drab : Oh for a commodious Drabb betwixt 'em ! wou'd *Hellen* had been here ! then it had come to ſomething. Dogs, Lyons, Bulls, for Females tear and gore : And the Beaſt Man , is valiant for his whore.   *Exit Therſites.*

ACT III. SCENE I.

Enter Therſites.

Therſ. SHall the Idiot *Ajax* uſe me thus ! he beats me and I rail at him: O worthy ſatisfaction ! wou'd I cou'd beat him, and he ra il'd at me ! Then there's *Achilles*, a rare Engineer : if *Troy* be not taken till theſe two undermine it, the walls will ſtand till they fall of themſelves : Now the Plague on the whole Camp, or rather the Pox : for that's a curſe dependent on thoſe that fight as we do for a Cuckolds queen.——— What ho, my Lord *Achilles.*

Enter Patroclus.

Patroc. Who's there, *Therſites* ! Good *Therſites* come in and rail.

Thers. aſide. If I cou'd have remembred an Aſſe with gilt trappings, thou hadſt not ſlip'd out of my contemplation. But 'tis no matter ; thy ſelf upon thy ſelf : the common curſe of mankiud, folly and ignorance be thine in great abundance : Heavens bleſſe thee from a Tutor ; and diſcipline come not near thee.

I have ſaid my prayers ; and the devil Envy ſay Amen.

Where's *Achilles* !

Enter Achilles.

Who's there *Therfites* ! why my digeſtion, why haſt thou not ſerv'd thy ſelf to my table, ſo many meals ! come begin what's *Agamemnon*?.

Thers. Thy Commander, *Achilles :* then tell me *Patroclus*, what's *Achilles ?*

Patro. Thy Benefactor *Therfites* ; then tell me prithee what's thy ſelf ?

Thers. Thy knower, *Patroclus* ; then tell me, *Patroclus*, what art thou ?

Patroc. Thou mayſt tell that know'ſt.

Achill. O, tell, tell. This muſt be very fooliſh : aud I dye to have my ſpleen tickled.

Thers. I'le decline the whole queſtion. *Agamemnon* commands *Achilles*, *Achilles* is my Benefactor, I am *Patroclus* knower ; and *Patroclus* is a fool.

Patroc. You Raſcal ?

Achill. He's a priviledg'd man, proceed *Therfites*. Ha ! ha ! ha ! prithee proceed while I am in the vein of laughing.

Therfit. And all theſe foreſaid men are fools : *Agamemnon's* a fool to offer to command *Achilles* : *Achilles* is a fool to be commanded by him, I am a fool to ſerve ſuch a fool, and *Patroclus* is a fool poſitive.

Patroc. Why am I a fool ?

Therfi. Make that demand to Heaven, it ſuffices me thou art one.

Achill. Ha, ha, ha ! O give me ribs of ſteel, or I ſhall ſplit with pleaſure: now play me *Neſtor* at a Night alarm : Mimick him rarely, make him cough and ſpet, and fumble with his gorget, and ſhake the rivits with his palſey hand ; in and out, in and out, gad that's exceeding fooliſh.

Patroc. *Neſtor* ſhall not ſcape ſo, he has told us what we are ; come what's *Neſtor* ?

Therfi. Why he's an old wooden top, ſet up by father Time three hundred years ago, that hums to *Agamemnon* and *Ulyſſes*, and ſleeps to all the world beſides.

Achill. So let him ſleep for I'le no more of him : O my *Patroclus*, I but force a ſmile, *Ajax* has drawn the lot, and all the praiſe of *Hector* muſt be his.

Therfi. I hope to ſee his praiſe upon his ſhoulders, in blows and bruiſes, his arms, thighs, and body, all full of fame ; ſuch fame as he gave me, and a wide hole at laſt full in his boſome, to let in day upon him, and diſcover the inſide of a fool.

Patroc. How he ſtruts in expectation of honour ! he knows not what he does.

Therfi. Nay that's no wonder, for he never did.

Achill. Prithee ſay how he behaves himſelf ?

Therfi. O you would be learning to practice, againſt ſuch another time.

E

time.——Why he toſſes up his head as he had built Caſtles ith' ayr ; and he treads upward to 'em, ſtalks into th' Element, he ſurveys him- ſelf, as 'twere to look for *Ajax* : he wou'd be cry'd, for he has loſt himſelf, nay he knows no body ; I ſaid good morrow *Ajax*, and he replyed thanks *Agamemnon*.

Achill. Thou ſhalt be my Ambaſſador to him *Therſites*.

Therſ. No, I'le put on his perſon, let *Patroclus* make his demands to me, and you ſhall ſee the pageant of *Ajax*.

Achill. To him *Patroclus*, tell him I humbly deſire the valiant *Ajax* to invite the Noble *Hector* to my Tent : and to procure ſafe conduct for him from our Captain General *Agamemnon*.

Patroc. *Jove* bleſs the mighty *Ajax* !

Therſi. Humh !

Patroc. I come from the great *Achilles*.

Therſi. Ha *!*

Patroc. Who moſt humbly deſires you to invite *Hector* to his Tent.

Therſi. Humh !

Patroc. And to procure him ſafe conduct from *Agamemnon*.

Therſi. *Agamemnon* ?

Patroc. I, my Lord.

Therſi. Ha !

Patro. What ſay you to 't ?

Therſi. Farewell with all my heart.

Patroc. Your anſwer Sir !

Therſi. If to morrow be a fair day, by eleven a clock it will go one way or tother, however he ſhall buy me dearly, fare you well with all my heart.

Achill. Why but he is not in this tune is he ?

Therſi. No, but he's thus out of tune, what Muſick will be in him when *Hector* has knocked out his brains I know not, nor I care not , but if emptineſs makes noiſe, his head will make melody.

Achill. My minde is troubled like a Fountain ſtir'd :
And I my ſelf ſee not the bottom on 't.

Therſi. Wou'd the Fountain of his minde were clear ; that he might ſee an Aſs in 't. [*Aſide.*] I had rather be a tick in a ſheep, than ſuch a valiant ignorance.

Enter Agamemnon, Ajax, Diomedes, Menelaus.

Patroc. Look who comes here.

Achill. *Patroclus*, I'le ſpeak with no body, come in after me *Therſites*.

Agam. Where's *Achilles* !   [*Exeunt* Achill. Therſites.

Patro. Within, but ill diſpos'd my Lord.

Menel. We ſaw him at the opening of his Tent.

Agam. Let it be known to him that we are here.

Patroc. I ſhall ſay ſo to him.   [*Exit* Patroclus.
                                                                    Diom,

Diom. I know he is not fick.

Ajax. Yes, Lyon fick, fick of a proud heart, you may call it melancholy if yo'll humour him : but on my honour 'tis no more than pride :
aud why fhou'd he be proud ?

Menel. Here comes *Patroclus* ; but no *Achilles* with him.

Enter Patroclus.

Patroc. Achilles bids me tell you he is forry
If any thing more than your fport and pleafure
Did move you to this vifit : he's not well,
And begs you wou'd excufe him, as unfit
For prefent bufinefs.

Agam. How *!* how's this *Patroclus* ?
We are too well acquainted with thefe anfwers.
Though he has much defert, yet all his vertues
Do in our eyes begin to lofe their glofs.
We came to fpeak with him ; you fhall not erre
If you return we think him over-proud
And under-honeft. Tell him this ; and adde,
That if he over-hold his price fo much
We'll none of him : but let him like an Engine
Not portable, lye lagg of all the Camp.
A ftirring Dwarf is of more ufe to us
Then is a fleeping Gyant : tell him fo.

Patroc. I fhall ; and bring his anfwer prefently.

Agam. I'le not be fatisfi'd but by himfelf.
So tell him, *Menelaus.*   *Exeunt Menelaus. Patroclus.*

Ajax. What's he more than another ?

Agam. No more than what he thinks himfelf.

Ajax. Is he fo much *!* do you not think he thinks himfelf a better
Man than me ?

Diom. No doubt he does.

Ajax. Do you think fo ?

Agam. No, noble *Ajax* ; you are as ftrong, as valiant ; but much
more courteous.

Ajax. Why fhou'd a man be proud ? *I* know not what pride is : I hate
a proud man as I hate the ingendring of toads.

Diom. Afide. 'Tis ftrange he fhould ; and love himfelf fo well.

Re-enter Menel.

Men. Achilles will not to the field to morrow.

Agam. What's his excufe ?

Men. Why he relies on none
But his own will ; poffeft he is with vanity :
What fhou'd I fay, he is fo plaguy proud
That the death tokens of it are upon him ;
And bode there's no recovery.

Enter Ulyſſes, Neſtor.

Agam. Let *Ajax* go to him.

Ulyſſ. O *Agamemnon*, let it not be ſo.
We'll conſecrate the ſteps that *Ajax* makes
When they go from *Achilles* : ſhall that proud man
Be worſhip'd by a greater than himſelf,
One whom we hold our Idoll ;
Shall *Ajax* go to him ? No, *Jove* forbid,
And ſay in thunder, go to him *Achilles*.

Neſt. [*Aſide.*] O, this is well ; he rubbs him where it itches.

Ajax. If I go to him with my Gantlet clench'd,
I'le daſh him or'e the face.

Agam. O no, you ſhall not go.

Ajax. And he be proud with me I'le cure his pride : a paltry
Inſolent fellow !

Neſt. How he deſcribes himſelf?

Ulyſſ. *Aſide.* The crow chides blackneſs.——here is a man, but 'tis
before his face, and therefore I am ſilent.

Neſt. Wherefore are you ? He is not envious as *Achilles* is.

Ulyſſ. Know all the world he is as valiant.

Ajax. A whorſon dogg that ſhall palter thus with us ! wou'd a
were a *Trojan*.

Ulyſſ. Thank Heav'n my Lord, you're of a gentle nature,
Praiſe him that got you, her that brought you forth ;
But he who taught you firſt the uſe of Armes,
Let *Mars* divide Eternity in two,
And give him half. I will not praiſe your wiſedome.
Neſtor ſhall do't ; but pardon father *Neſtor*,
Were you as green as *Ajax*, and your brain
Temper'd like his, you never ſhou'd excell him ;
But be as *Ajax* is.

Ajax. Shall I call you father ?

Ulyſſ. I, my good Son.

Diom. Be rul'd by him Lord *Ajax*.

Ulyſſ. There is no ſtaying here ; the Hart *Achilles*
Keeps thicket, pleaſe it our great General.
I ſhall impart a counſell, which obſerv'd
May cure this Madmans pride.

Agam. In my own tent our talk will be more private.

Ulyſſ. But nothing without *Ajax* :
He is the ſoul and ſubſtance of my councels
And I am but his ſhadow.

Ajax. You ſhall ſee
I am not like *Achilles*,
Let us confer ; and I'le give counſel too.

[*Exeunt Omnes.*
SCENE

SCENE II.

Pandarus, Troilus, Creſſida.

Pand. Come, come, what need you bluſh ? ſhame's a babie ; ſwear the oaths now to her, that you ſwore to me : what are you gone again ? you muſt be watch'd ere you are made tame muſt you ? why don't you ſpeak to her firſt ! ——Come draw this Curtain, and lets ſee your picture : alas a day, how loath you are to offend day-light !——(they kiſſe) that's well, that's well, nay you ſhall fight your hearts out ere I part you.——ſo ſo——ſo ſo——

Troil. You have bereft me of all words, fair *Creſſida.*

Pand. Words, pay no debts ; give her deeds :——what billing again ! here's in witneſs whereof the parties interchangeably —— come in, come in, you loſe time both.

Troil. O *Creſſida,* how often have I wiſh'd me here ?

Creſſi. Wiſh'd my Lord !——the Gods grant ! O my Lord.——

Troil. What ſhou'd they grant ? what makes this pretty interrupti-on in thy words ?

Creſſi. I ſpeak I know not what !

Troil. Speak ever ſo ; and if I anſwer you I know not what, it ſhews the more of love. Love is a child that talks in broken language, Yet then he ſpeaks moſt plain.

Creſs. I finde it true, that to be wiſe and love Are inconſiſtent things.

Pand. what bluſhing ſtill, have you not done talking yet !

Creſs. Well Unkle, what folly I commit, I dedicate to you.

Pand. I thank you for that : if my Lord get a boy of you, you'l give him me. Be true to my Lord, if he flinch Ile be hang'd for him——— (Now am I in my kingdome ! [*aſide*]

Troil. You know your pledges now , your Unkles word and my firm faith.

Pand. Nay Ile give my word for her too : our kindred are conſtant : they are burrs I can aſſure you, they'll ſtick where they are thrown.

Creſs. Boldneſs comes to me now, and I can ſpeak : Prince *Troylus,* I have lov'd you long.

Troil. Why was my *Creſſida* then ſo hard to win ?

Creſs. Hard to ſeem wonn ; but I was wonn my Lord. What have I blabb'd, who will be true to us, When we are ſo unfaithfull to our ſelves ! O bid me hold my tongue ? for in this rapture Sure I ſhall ſpeak what I ſhou'd ſoon repent. But ſtop my mouth.

Troil.

Troil. A sweet command; and willingly obey'd.

Pand. Pretty I faith!   [*kisses*]

Cress. My Lord I do beseech you pardon me,
'Twas not my purpose thus to beg a kisse.
I am asham'd: O heavens what have I done!
For thts time let me take my leave, my Lord.

Pand, Leave! and you take leave till to morrow morning, call
me Cut.

Cress. Pray let me go.

Troil, Why what offends you, Madam?

Cress. My own company.

Troil. You cannot shun your self.

Cress. Let me go and try:
I have a kind of self resides in you.

Troil. Oh that I thought truth cou'd be in a woman!
(As if it can, I will presume in you)
That my integrity and faith might meet
The same return from her who has my heart.
How shou'd I be exaltted! but alas
I am more plain then dull simplicity!
And art less, as the infancy of truth.

Cress. In that I must not yield to you my Lord.

Troil. All constant Lovers shall, in future Ages,
Approve their truth by *Troylus:* when their verse
Wants *similes,* as turtles to their mates:
Or true as flowing tides are to the Moon;
Earth to the Center: Iron to Adamant:
At last when truth is tir'd with repetition;
As true as *Troylus* shall crown up the verse,
And sanctify the Numbers.

Cress. Prophet may you be!
If I am false, or swerve from truth of love,
When time is old, and has forgot it self,
In all things else, let it remember me;
And after all comparisons of falshood
To stabb the heart of perjury in Maids;
Let it be said as false as *Cressida.*

Pand. Go to, little ones: a bargain made: here I hold your hand, and
here my Cousins: if ever you prove false to one another, after I have
taken such pains to bring you together: let all pitifull goers between,
be call'd to the worlds end after my name, *Pandars.*

Cress. And will you promise that the holy Priest
Shall make us one for ever!

Pand.

Pand. Priests! marry hang 'em *!* they make you one *!* go in, go in, and make your selves one without a priest : I'le have no priests work in my house.

Cress. Ile not consent unless you swear.

Pand. I, do, do, swear ; a pretty woman's worth an oath at any time. Keep or break as time shall try ; but 'tis good to swear, for the saving of her credit *:* Hang e'm sweet Rogues they never expect a Man shou'd keep it. Let him but swear, and that's all they care for.

Troil. Heavens prosper me as I devoutly swear,
Never to be but yours.

Pand. Whereupon I will lead you into a chamber : and suppose there be a bed in't ; as I fack, I know not : but you'll forgive me, if there be : away, away, you naughty hildings : get ye together, get you together. Ah you wags, do you leer indeed at one another *!* do the neyes twinkle at him ! get you together, get you together.

[Leads them out.

Enoter at one door Æneas with a Torch, at another Hector,
Diomede with Torches,

Hect. So ho ; who goes there ? *Æneas !*

Æneas. Prince *Hector !*

Diom. Good morrow Lord *Æneas.*

Hect. A valiant Greek, *Æneas* ; take his hand ;
Witnesse the processe of your speech within ;
You told how *Diomede* a whole week by days
Did haunt you in the field.

Æneas. Health to you, valiant Sir,
During all business of the gentle truce ;
But when I meet you arm'd, as black defiance
As heart can think, or courage execute.

Diom. Both one and to'ther, *Diomede* embraces.
Our bloods are now in calm ; and so, long health ;
But when contention, and occasion meets,
By *Jove* I'le play the hunter for thy life,

Eneas. And thou shalt hunt a Lyou that will fly
With his face backward : welcome *Diomede*
Welcome to *Troy* : now by *Anchises* Soul
No man alive can love in such a sort
The thing he means to kill, more excellently.

Diom. We know each other well.

Æne. We do ; and long to know each other worse
To *Hect.* my Lord, the King has sent for me in haste :
Know you the reason ?

Hect. Yes : his purpose meets you.
It was to bring this *Greek* to *Colchas's* house,

Where

Where *Pandarus* his Brother, and his Daughter
Fair *Creffida* refide : and there to render
For our *Anthenor*, now redeem'd from prifon,
The Lady *Creffida* :

Æne. What *!* Has the King refolv'd to gratifie
That Traytor *Colchos* ; who forfook his Country,
And turn'd to them, by giving up this pledge ?

Hect. The bitter difpofition of the time
Is fuch, though *Colchos* as a fugitive
Deferve it not, that we muft free *Anthenor*
On whofe wife Counfels, we can moft rely :
And therefore *Creffida* muft be return'd.

Æne. A word my Lord——(Your pardon *Diomede*)
Your Brother *Troylus*, to my certain knowledg,
Does lodge this night in *Paudarus* his houfe :

Hect. Go you before : tell him of our approach
Which will I fear be much
Unwelcome to him.

Æne. I affure you
Troylus had rather *Troy* were born to *Greece*
Than *Creffida* from *Troy*.

Hect. I know it well : and how he is befide,
Of hafty blood :

Æne. He will not hear me fpeak :
But I have noted long betwixt you two
A more than Brothers love : an awfull homage
The fiery youth pays to your elder vertue.

Hect. Leave it to me ; l'le manage him alone :
Attend you *Diomede* ; My Lord good morrow :   [to *Diomed.*
An urgent bufinefs takes me from the pleafure
Your company affords me ; but *Æneas*
With joy will undertake to ferve you here,
And to fupply my room.

    Æneas to Diomed. My Lord I wait you.   *Exeunt feverally.*
        [Diomede *with* Æneas ; Hector *at another door.*
      Enter Pandarus : *a Servant* : *Mufick.*

Pand. Softly, villain, foftly ; I would not for half *Troy* the Lovers fhould be difturb'd under my roof ; liften rogue, liften, do they
breathe ?

Serv. Yes, Sir, I hear by fome certain fignes, the are both awaken.

Pand. That's as it fhou'd be : that's well aboth fides :   [*liftens*]
Yes faith they are both alive :———there was a creake ! there was a
creake : they are both alive and alive like ; there was a creake : a ha
boyes !——Is the mufick ready ?

                                            Serv.

Serv. Shall they ſtrike up Sir!

Pand. Art thou ſure they do not know the parties?

Serv. They play to the Man in the Moon for ought they know.

Pand. To the Man in the Moon, ah Rogue! do they ſo indeed Rogue! I underſtand, thee: thou art a wag; thou art a wagg. Come towze rowze! in the name of love, ſtrike up boys!

Muſick: and then Song: during which Pandarus liſtens.

Song. *CAn life be a bleſſing,*
Or worth the poſſeſſing,
Can life be a bleſſing if love were away?
Ah no! though our love all night keep us waking,
And though he torment us with cares all the day,
Yet he ſweetens he ſweetens our pains in the taking,
There's an hour at the laſt, there's an hour to repay.

2.

In every poſſeſſiug,
The raviſhing bleſſing,
In every poſſeſſing the fruit of our pain,
Poor lovers forget long ages of anguiſh,
Whate're they have ſuffer'd and done to obtain;
'Tis a pleaſure, a pleaſure to ſigh and to languiſh,
When we hope, when we hope to be happy again.

Pand. Put up, and vaniſh; they are coming out; what a ferrup, will you play when the dance is done? I ſay vaniſh.   *Exit Muſick.*

Peeping. Good Ifaith; good ifarth! what hand in hand!——— a fair quarrell, well ended! do, do, walk him, walk him; A good girl, a diſcreet girl: I ſee ſhe'll make the moſt of him.

Enter Troil. *and* Creſſida.

Troil. Farewell, my life! leave me and back to bed: Sleep ſeal thoſe pretty eyes; And tye thy ſences in as ſoft a band As Infants voyd of thought.

Pandar. ſhewing himſelf. How now, how now, how go matters! hear you Maid, hear you; where's my Couſin *Creſſida?*

Creſs. Go hang your ſelf you naughty mocking Unkle: You bring me to do ill and then you jeere me!

Pand. What ill have I brought you to do? ſay what if you dare now! My Lord have I brought her to do ill?

Creſs. Come, come, beſhrew your heart; you'll neither be good your ſelf, nor ſuffer others.

F

Pand.

Pand. Alas poor wench ; alas poor Devil ; haſt not ſlept to night ? wou'd anot (a naughty Man) let it ſleep one twinkle! Ah bugbear take him !

Knock within. *Creſs.* Who's that at door ? good Uncle go and ſee : My Lord come you again into my chamber ! You ſmile and mock as if I meant naughtily !

Troil. Indeed, indeed !

Creſs. Come y'are deceiv'd ; I think of no ſuch thing :

Knock again. How earneſtly they knock, pray come in : I wou'd not for all *Troy,* you were ſeen here. [*Exeunt Troil. Creſſida.*

Pand. Who's there ! whats the matter ! Will you beat down the houſe there !

Enter Hector.

Hect. Good morrow my Lord *Pandarus* ; good morrow !

Pand. Who's there, Prince *Hector* ! what news with you ſo early ?

Hect. Is not my Brother *Troilus* here ?

Pand. Here ! what ſhou'd he do here ?

Hect. Come he is here my Lord, do not deny him : It does import him much to ſpeak with me.

Pand. Is he here ſay you ? 'tis more than I know, I'le be ſworn ! For my own part I came in late !——what ſhou'd he do here ?

Hect. Come, come you do him wrong ere y'are aware ; you'll be ſo true to him, that you'll be falſe to him : you ſhall not know he's here ; but yet go fetch him hither :—goe. [*Exit* Pandarus.

Enter Troilus.

Hect. I bring you Brother, moſt unwelcome news ; But ſince of force you are to hear it told, I thought a friend and Brother beſt might tell it : Therefore, before I ſpeak, arm well your mind And think y'are to be touch'd ev'n to the quick ; That ſo, prepar'd for ill you may be leſs Surpris'd to hear the worſt.

Troil. See *Hector,* what it is to be your Brother, I ſtand prepar'd already.

Hect. Come, you are not, I know you *Troilus,* you are hot and fiery : You kindle at a wrong ; and catch it quick As ſtubble does the flame.

Troil. 'Tis heat of blood And raſhneſs of my youth ; I'le mend that errour : Begin and try my temper.

Hect. Can you think Of that one thing which moſt cou'd urge your anger Drive you to madneſs, plague you on diſpair,

And

And make you hate ev'n me?

Troil. There can be nothing.
I love you Brother, with that awful love
I bear to Heav'n, and to superior vertue,
And when I quit this love you must be that
Which *Hector* near can be.

Hect. Remember well
What you have said: for when I claim your promise
I shall expect performance.

Troil. I am taught:
I will not rage.

Hect. Nor grieve beyond a man.

Troil. I won'not be a woman.

Hect. Do not Brother:
And I will tell my news, in terms so mild,
So tender, and so fearful to offend
As Mothers use to sooth their froward Babes;
Nay I will swear as you have sworn to me,
That if some gust of passion swell your soul
To words intemperate, I will bear with you.

Troil. What wou'd this pomp of preparation mean?
Come you to bring me news of *Priams* death
Or *Hecuba*'s.

Hect. The Gods forbid I shou'd:
But what I bring is nearer you, more close,
An ill more yours.

Troil. There is but one that can be.

Hect. Perhaps 'tis that.

Troil. I'le not suspect my fate
So far, I know i stand possest of that.

Hect. 'Tis well: consider at whose house I finde you.

Troil. Ha!

Hect. Does it start you! I must wake you more:
Anthenor is exchang'd.

Troil. For whom.

Hect. Imagine.

Troil. It comes like thunder grumbling in a cloud,
Before the dreadfull break: if here it fall,
The subtile flame will lick up all my blood,
And in a moment turn my heart to ashes.

Hect. That *Cressida* for *Anthenor* is exchang'd
Because knew 'twas harsh I wou'd not tell;
Not all at once; but by degrees and glimpses
I let it in, lest it might rush upon you
And quite orepower your Soul: in this I think

F 2

I fhow'd a friend : your part muft follow next :
Which is, to curb your choler, tame your grief,
And bear it like a man.

   Troil. I think I do
That I yet live to hear you : but no more :
Hope for no more: for fhou'd fome Goddefs offer
To give her felf and all her Heaven in change,
I wou'd not part with *Creffida* : fo return
This anfwer as my laft.

   Hect. 'Twill not be taken:
Nor will I bear fuch news.

   Troil. You bore me worfe.

   Hect. Worfe for your felf; not for the general ftate,
And all our common fafety, which depends
On free'd *Anthenors* wifdome.

   Troil. Yon wou'd fay
That I'm the Man mark'd out to be unhappy ;
And made the publick Sacrifice for *Troy.*

   Hect. I wou'd fay fo indeed : for can you finde
A fate more glorious than to be that victime ?
If parting from a Miftrifs can procure
A Nations happinefs, fhow me that Prince
Who dares to truft his future fame fo farr
To ftand the fhock of Annals, blotted thus
He fold his Country for a womans love ?

   Troil. O, fhe's my life, my being, and my Soul !

   Hect. Suppofe fhe were, which yet I will not grant,
You ought to give her up.

   Troil. For whom !

   Hect. The publick.

   Troil. And what are they that I fhou'd give up her
To make them happy ? let me tell you Brother,
The publick , is the Lees of vulgar flaves :
Slaves, with the minds of flaves : fo born, fo bred :
Yet fuch as thefe united in a herd
Are call'd the publique : Millions of fuch Cyphers
Make up the publique fum : an Eagles life
Is worth a world of Crows : are Princes made
For fuch as thefe, who, were one Soul extracted
From all their beings, cou'd not raife a Man.——

   Hect. And what are we, but for fuch men as thefe ?
'Tis adoration, fome fay makes a God :
And who fhou'd pay it, where wou'd be their Altars
Were no inferiour creatures here on Earth ?
Ev'n thofe who ferve have their expectances ;

Degrees

Degrees of happiness, which they muſt ſhare,
Or they'll refuſe to ſerve us.

Troil. Let e'm have it.
Let e'm eat, drink and ſleep ; the only uſe
They have of life :

Hect. You take all theſe away,
Unleſs you give up *Creſſida.*

Troil. Forbear ;
Let *Paris* give up *Hellen* : ſhe's the cauſe,
And root of all this miſchief.

Hect. Your own ſuffrage
Condemns you there : you voted for her ſtay.

Troil. If one muſt ſtay, the other ſha'not go.

Hect. She ſha'not ?

Troil. Once again, I ſay ſhe ſhall not.

Hect. Our Father has decree'd it otherwiſe.

Troil. No matter.

Hect. How ! no matter *Troylus ?*
A King, and fathers will !

Troil. When 'tis unjuſt.

Hect. Come ſhe ſhall go.

Troil. She ſhal ? then I am dar'd.

Hect. If nothing elſe will do.

Troil. Anſwer me firſt ;
And then Ile anſwer that : be ſure I will ;
Whoſe hand ſeal'd this exchange ?

Hect. My Fathers firſt ;
Then all the Council's after.

Troil. Was yours there ?

Hect. Mine was there too.

Troil. Then you'r no more my friend :
And for your ſake now mark me what I ſay,
She ſhall not go.

Hect. Go to, you are a boy.

Troil. A Boy ! Im'e glad I am not ſuch a Man,
Not ſuch as thou ; a traytor to thy Brother :
Nay more, thy friend : but friend's a Sacred name,
Which none but brave and honeſt men ſhou'd wear ;
In thee 'tis vile ; 'tis proſtitute : 'tis Ayr ;
And thus I puffe it from me.

Hect. Well, young Man,
Since I'me no friend (and oh that ere I was
To one ſo far unworthy) bring her out,
Or by our Fathers Soul, of which no part
Did ere deſcend to thee, Ile force her hence.

Troil. I laugh at thee.

Hect. Thou dar'ft not.

Troil. I dare more,
If urg'd beyond my temper: prove my daring,
And fee which of us has the larger fhare.
Of our great Fathers Soul.

Hect. No more, thou knowft me.

Troil. I do ; and know my felf.

Hect. All this ye Gods,
And for the Daughter of a fugitive,
A Traytor to his Country !

Troil. 'Tis too much.

Hect. By Heaven too little ; for I think her common,

Troil. How, Common !

Hect. Common as the tainted fhambles,
Or as the duft we tread.

Troil. By Heaven as chafte as thy *Andromaohe.*

> Hector *lays his hand on* Troylus *his Arm ;*
> *and* Troylus *does the fame to him.*

Hect. What ! nam'ft thou them together !

Troil. No ; I do not :
For *Creffida* is firft : as chafte as fhe,
But much more fair.

Hect. O patience, patience, Heaven !
Thou tempt'ft me ftrangely : fhou'd I kill thee now,
I know not if the Gods can be offended
Or think I flew a Brother; but be gone,
Be gone, or I fhall fhake thee into Atomes :
Thou know'ft I can.

Troil. I care not if you cou'd.

Hect. walking off. I thank ye Gods for calling to my minde
My promife that no words of thine fhou'd urge me,
Beyond the bounds of reafon : But in thee
'Twas brutall bafenefs, fo forewarn'd to fall
Beneath the name of man : to fpurn my kindnefs ;
And when offer'd thee (thou knowft how loth !)
The wholfome bitter cup o' friendly counfel
To dafh it in my face : farewel, farewel.
Ungratefull as thou art : hereafter ufe
The name of Brother ; but of friend no more.   [*going out.*

Troil. Wilt thou not break yet heart? ftay Brother, ftay.
I promis'd too, but I have broke my vow,
And you keep yours too well.

Hect.

Hect. What wouldst thou more ?
Take heed, young man how you too far provoke me!
For Heaven can witness 'tis with much constraint
That I preserve my faith.
   Troil. Else you wou'd kill me;
   Hect. By all the Gods I wou'd.
   Troil. I'me satisfi'd.
You have condemn'd me, and Ile do't my self;
What's life to him, who has no use of life ?
A barren purchase, held upon hard terms!
For I have lost (oh what have I not lost !)
The fairest, dearest, kindest of her Sex,
And lost her ev'n by him, by him, ye Gods,
Who only cou'd, and only shou'd protect me!
And if I had a joy beyond that love,
A friend, have lost him too!
   Hect. Speak that again:
(For I cou'd hear it ever :) saidst thou not
That if thou hadst a joy beyond that love
It was a friend ? O saydst thou not a friend !
That doubting if was kinde : then thou'rt divided;
And I have still some part,
   Troil. If still you have
You do not care to have it.
   Hect. How, not care!
   Troil. No, Brother, care not.
   Hect. Am I but thy Brother !
   Troil. You told me I must call you friend no more.
   Hect. How far my words were distant from my heart!
Know when I told thee so I lov'd thee most.
Alas ! it is the use of human frailty
To fly to worst extremities with those
To whom we most are kind.
   Troil. Is't possible !
Then you are still my friend !
   Hect. Heaven knows I am !
   Troil. And can forgive the Sallies of my passion ?
For I have been too blame : oh much too blame :
Have said such words, nay done such actions too,
(Base as am) that my aw'd, conscious Soul
Sinks in my breast, nor dare I lift an eye
On him I have offended.
   Hect. Peace be to thee
And calmness ever there. I blame thee not:

                                        I know

I know thou lov'ſt ; and what can love not do !
I caſt the wild diſorderly account
Of all thy words and deeds on that mad paſſion ;
I pity thee, indeed I pity thee :

    Troil. Do ; for I need it : let me lean my head
Upon thy boſome ; all my peace dwells there ;
Thou art ſome God, or much much more then man !

    Hect. Alas ! to loſe the joys of all thy youth,
One who deſerv'd thy love !

    Troil, Did ſhe deſerve ?

    Hect. She did.

    Troil. Then ſure ſhe was no common creature.

    Hect. I ſaid it in my rage, I thought not ſo.

    Troil. That thought has bles'd me ! but to loſe this love
After long pains, and after ſhort poſſeſſion.

    Hect. I feel it for thee : Let me go to *Priam*,
I'le break this treaty off ; or let me fight ;
I'le be thy champion ; and ſecure both her
And thee, and *Troy.*

    Troil. It muſt not be, my Brother !
For then your errour would be more then mine :
I'le bring her forth, and you ſhall bear her hence ;
That you have pitied me is my reward.

    Hect. Go then ; and the good gods reſtore her to thee,
And with her all the quiet of thy minde ;
The triumph of this kindeneſs be thy own ;

    And heaven and earth this teſtimony yield,
    That Friendſhip never gain'd a nobler field.   *Exeunt ſeverally.*

A CT.

ACT IV. SCENE I.

Enter Pandarus, Creſſida *meeting.*

Pand. I'St poſſible ! no ſooner got but loſt !
The devil take *Antenor* : the young Prince will go mad :
A plague upon *Anthenor !* wou'd they had broke's neck.

Creſſi. How now ! what's the matter ! who was here !

Pand. Oh, oh !

Creſſi. Why ſigh you ſo ! O where's my *Troilus* ? tell me ſweet
Uncle what's the matter ?

Pand. Wou'd I were as deep under the earth, as I am above it !

Creſſi. Oh the Gods, what's the matter ?

Pand. Prithee get thee in, wou'd thou hadſt never been born !
I knew thou woud'ſt be his death ; oh poor Gentleman !
A plague upon *Antenor ?*

Creſſi. Good Uncle, I beſeech you on my knees, tell me what's the
matter ?

Pand. Thou muſt be gone girl ; thou muſt be gone, to the fugitive
Rogue Prieſt thy father, (and he's my brother too, but that's all one
at this time :) a pox upon *Antenor.* ?

Creſſi. O ye immortal Gods, i will not go.

Pand. Thou muſt, thou muſt ?

Creſſi. I will not : I have quite forgot my father ;
I have no touch of birth ; no ſpark of Nature :
No kinn, no blood, no life ; nothing ſo near me
As my dear *Troilus?*

Enter Troilus.

Pand. Here, here, here, he comes ſweet Duck !

Creſſi. O *Troilus, Troilus* !   [*They both weep over each other, ſhe
running into his armes.*

Pand. What a pair of Spectacles is here ! let me embrace too : Oh
heart, *ſings* (as the ſaying is) O heart, heavy heart, why ſighſt thou
without breaking (where he anſwers again) becauſe thou canſt not
eaſe thy ſmart, by friendſhip nor by ſpeaking, there was never a truer
rhime ; let us caſt away nothing ; for we may live to have need of ſuch
a verſe : we ſee it, we ſee it, how now lambs ?

Troil. Creſſida, I love thee with ſo ſtrange a purity
That the bleſt Gods, angry with my devotions
More bright in zeal, than that I pay their Altars,
Will take thee from my ſight ?

Creſſi. Have the Gods envy ?

Pand. I, I, i, 'tis too plain a caſe !

G

Creſſi. And is it true, that I muſt go from *Troy*?

Troil. A haſtefull truth?

Creſſi. What, and from *Troilus* too?

Troil. From *Troy* and *Troilus* : and ſuddenly.
So ſuddenly 'tis counted but by minutes.

Creſſi. What not an hour allow'd for taking leave?

Troil. Ev'n that's bereft us too : our envious fates
Juſtle betwixt, and part the dear adieus
Of meeting lips, claſp'd hands, and lock'd embraces.

Æneas within.

My Lord, is the Lady ready yet?

Troil. Hark, you are call'd : ſome ſay the Genius ſo
Cryes come, to him who inſtantly muſt dye.

Pand. Where are my tears! ſome rain to'lay this wind:
Or my heart will be blown up by th' roots!

Troil. Hear me my Love! be thou but true like me.

Creſſi. I true! how now, what wicked thought is this?

Troil. Nay, we muſt uſe expoſtulation kindly,
For it is parting from us:
I ſpoke not, be thou true, as fearing thee;
But be thou true, I ſaid to introduce
My following proteſtation : be thou true,
And I will ſee thee.

Creſſi. You'll be expos'd to dangers.

Troil. I care not : but be true.

Creſſi. Be true again?

Troil. Hear why I ſpeak it love.
The *Grecian* Youths are full of *Grecian* Arts :
Alas a kind of holy jealouſie
Which I beſeech you call a vertuous ſin,
Makes me afraid how far you may be tempted.

Creſſi. O Heavens, you love me not!

Troil Dye I, a villain then!
In this I do not call your faith in queſtion
But my own merit.

Creſſi. Fear not; I'le be true.

Troil. Then fate thy worſt; for I will ſee thee love
Not all the *Grecian* hoſt ſhall keep me out,
Nor *Troy*, though wall'd with fire, ſhou'd hold me in.

Æneas within.

My Lord, my Lord *Troilus* : I muſt call you.

Pand. A miſchief call him : nothing but Schreechowls? do, do, call
again; you had beſt part 'em now in the ſweetneſſe of their love! I'le
be hang'd if this *Æneas* be the Son of *Venus*, for all his bragging.

Honeſt

Honeſt *Venus* was a Punk: wou'd ſhe have parted Lovers : no he has not
a drop of *Venus* blood in him : honeſt *Venus* was a Punk.

Troil. To *Pand.* Prithee go out ; and gain one minute more.

Pand. Marry and I will: follow you your buſineſs ; loſe no time, 'tis
very precious ; go, *Bill* again : I'le tell the Rogue his own I warrant
him.   [*Exit* Pandarus.

Creſſi. What have we gain'd by this one minute more ?

Troil. Only to wiſh another, and another
A longer ſtruggling with the pangs of death.

Creſſi. O thoſe who do not know what parting is
Can never learn to dye !

Troil. When I but think this ſight may be our laſt,
If *Jove* cou'd ſet me in the place of *Atlas*
And lay the weight of Heav'n and Gods upon me
He cou'd not preſſe me more.

Creſſi. Oh let me go that I may know my grief ;
Grief is but gueſs'd, while thou art ſtanding by :
But I too ſoon ſhall know what abſence is.

Troil. Why 'tis to be no more : another name for death.
'Tis the Sunn parting from the frozen North ;
And I, me thinks, ſtand on ſome Icey cliff,
To watch the laſt low circles that he makes ;
Till he ſink down from Heav'n ! O only *Creſſida*,
If thou depart from me, I cannot live :
I have not ſoul enough to laſt for grief,
But thou ſhalt hear what grief has done with me.

Creſſi. If I could live to hear it, I were falſe,
But as a careful traveller who fearing
Aſſaults of Robbers, leaves his wealth behind,
I truſt my heart with thee ; and to the *Greeks*
Bear but an empty Casket.

Troil. Then, I will live ; that I may keep that treaſure :
And arm'd with this aſſurance, let thee go
Looſe, yet ſecure as is the gentle Hawk
When whiſtled off ſhe mounts into the wind :
Our love's, like Mountains high above the clouds,
Though winds and tempeſts beat their aged feet,
Their peaceful heads nor ſtorm nor thunder know,
But ſcorn the threatning rack that roles below,
                                        Exeunt Ambo.

SCENE II.

Achilles *and* Patroclus, *standing in their Tent.*

Ulyſſes, Agamemnon, Menelaus, Neſtor, Ajax, *paſſing over the Stage.*

Ulyſs. A*Chilles* ſtands in th'entrance of his Tent :
    Pleaſe it our General to paſs ſtrangely by him,
As if he were forgot, and Princes all
Look on him with neglectful eyes and ſcorn :
Pride muſt be cur'd by pride.

  Agam. We'll execute your purpoſe, and put on
A form of ſtrangneſs as we paſs along
So do each Prince either ſalute him not
Or elſe diſdainfully, which will ſhake him more
Then if not look'd on : I will lead the way.

  Achill. What, comes the General to ſpeak with me !
You know my mind ; I'll fight no more with *Troy.*

  Agam. What ſays *Achilles,* wou'd he ought with us ?

  Neſt. Wou'd you, my Lord, ought with the General !

  Achill. No.

  Neſt. Nothing my Lord.

  Agam. The better.

  Menel. How do you, how do you !

  Achill. What does the Cuckold ſcorn me !

  Ajax. How now *Patroclus* !

  Achill. Good morrow *Ajax.*

  Ajax. Ha !

  Achill. Good morrow.

  Ajax. I ; and good next day too.

           [*Exeunt all but* Achilles, *and* Patroclus.

  Achill. What mean theſe fellows ! know they not *Achilles* ?

  Patroc. They paſs by ſtrangely ; they were us'd to bow ;
And ſend their ſmiles before 'em to *Achilles,*
To come as humbly as they us'd to creep, to holy Altars.

  Achill. Am I poor of late !
'Tis certain, greatneſs once fall'n out with fortune
Muſt fall out with men too ! what the declind is
He ſhall as ſoon read in the eyes of others
As feel in his own fall : for men like butter-flyes ;
Show not their mealy wings but to the Summer.

  Patroc. 'Tis known you are in love with *Hector's* Siſter,
And therefore will not fight : and your not fighting

                          Draws

Draws on you this contempt : I oft have told you
A woman impudent and mannifh grown
Is not more loath'd than an effeminate man,
In time of action : I'm condemn'd for this :
They think my little appetite to warr
Deads all the fire in you : but rowfe your felf,
And love fhall from your neck unloofe his folds ;
Or like a dew drop from a Lyons Mane
Be fhaken into ayr.

Achill. Shall *Ajax* fight with *Hector* ?
Patrocl. Yes, and perhaps fhall gain much honour by him.
Achill. I fee my reputation is at ftake.
Patroc. O then beware, thofe wounds heal ill that men have giv'n themfelves, becaufe they give e'm deepeft.
Achill. I'le do fomething :
But what I know not yet,——No more our Champion.

Re-enter Ajax, Agamemnon, Menelaus, Ulyffes, Neft. Diomede, Trumpet·

Agam. Here art thou daring combat, valiant *Ajax.*
Give with thy Trumpet, a loud note to *Troy,*
Thou Noble Champion, that the founding ayr
May pierce the ears of the great challenger,
And call him hither.

Ajax. Trumpet take that purfe :
Now crack thy lungs, and fplit the founding brafs ;
Thou blow'ft for *Hector.*

[*Trumpet founds, and is anfwer'd from within.*

Enter Hector, Æneas, *and other Trojans.*

Agam. Yonder comes the Troop.

Æneas, *coming to the Greeks.*

Health to the Grecian Lords; what fhall be done
To him that fhall be vanquifh'd ? or do you purpofe,
A Victor fhould be known ! will you the Knights,
Shall to the edg of all extremity,
Purfue each other, or fhall be divided
By any voice or order of the field ;
Hector bad ask.

Agam. Which way wou'd *Hector* have it ?
Æne. He cares not, he'll obey conditions.
Achill. 'Tis done like *Hector* but fecurely done ;
A little proudly, and too much difpifing
The Knight oppos'd, he might have found his match.
Æne. If not *Achilles,* Sir, what is your name !

Achill.

Achill. If not *Achilles* nothing.

Æne. Therefore *Achilles*, but who ere know this ;
Great *Hector* knows no pride, weigh him but well,
And that which looks like pride is courtefy.
This *Ajax* is half made of *Hectors* blood,
In love whereof half *Hector* ftays at home ;

Achill. A Maiden battle ! I perceive you then.

Agam. Go *Diomede*, and ftand by valiant *Ajax*:
As you and Lord *Æneas* fhall confent,
So let the fight proceed or terminate.

[*The Trumpets found on both fides, while* Æneas *and* Diomede *take their places, as Judges of the Field : The Trojans and Grecians rank themfelves on either fide.*

Ulyf. They are oppos'd already.

[*Fight equal at firft, then* Ajax *has* Hector *at difadvantage : at laft* Hector *clofes,* Ajax *falls on one knee,* Hector *ftands over him but ftriks not, and* Ajax *rifes.*

Æneas *throwing his Gantlet betwixt them.*

Princes enough, you both have fhown much valour.

Diomede. And we as Judges of the Field declare ;
The combat here fhall ceafe.

Ajax. I am not warm yet, let us fight again.

Æne. Then let it be as *Hector* fhall determine.

Hect. If it be left to me, I will no more.
Ajax, thou art my Aunt *Hefion's* Son ;
The Obligation of our blood forbids us.
But were thy mixture Greek and Trojan fo,
That thou cou'dft fay, this part is Grecian all
And this is Trojan, hence thou fhou'dft not bear
One Grecian limb, wherein my pointed Sword
Had not impreffion made, but Heav'n forbid
That any drop thou borrowft from my Mother,
Shou'd ere be draind by me, let me embrace thee Coufin :
By him who thunders thou haft finnewy arms,
Hector wou'd have 'em fall upon him thus :——[*Embrace*]
Thine be the honour, *Ajax*.

Ajax. I thank thee *Hector*,
Thou art too gentle, and too free a Man :
I came to kill thee Coufin, and to gain
A great addition from that glorious act :
But thou haft quite difarm'd me.

Hect. I am glad.

For 'tis the only way I cou'd difarm thee.

Ajax. If I might in intreaty finde fuccefs,
I wou'd defire to fee thee at my Tent.

Diom. 'Tis *Agamemnons* wifh, and great *Achilles*,
Both long to fee the valiant *Hector* there.

Hect. *Æneas*, call my Brother *Troilus* to me ;
And you two figne this friendly enterview.

          [Agamemnon, *and the chief of both fides approach,*

Agam. to *Hect.* Worthy of Arms, as welcome as to one
Who wou'd be rid of fuch an Enemy.

  To *Troil.* My well fam'd Lord of *Troy*, no lefs to you.

Neft. I have, thou gallant Trojan feen thee often
Labouring for deftiny, make cruel way,
Through ranks of Grecian youth, and I have feen thee
As fwift as lightning fpur thy *Phrygian* Steed,
And feen thee fcorning many forfeit lives,
When thou haft hung thy advanc'd Sword ith' ayr,
Not leting it decline, on proftrate foes :
That I have faid to all the ftanders by
Lo *Jove* is yonder, diftributing life.

Hect. Let me embrace thee, good old Chronicle,
Who haft fo long walkt hand in hand with time :
Moft Reverend *Neftor*, I am glad to clafp thee.

Ulyff. I wonder now, how yonder City ftands,
When we have here, her bafe and pillar by us.

  Hect. I know your count'nance, Lord *Ulyffes* well ;
Ah Sir, there's many a Greek and Trojan dead,
Since firft I faw your felf and *Diomede*,
In *Ilion*, on your Greekifh Embaffy.

Achill. Now *Hector*, I have fed mine eyes on thee ;
I have with exact view perus'd thee *Hector*,
And quoted joint by joint.

Hect. Is this *Achilles* !

Achill. I am *Achilles*.

Hect. Stand fair, I prithee let me look on thee.

Achill. Behold thy fill.

Hect. Nay, I have done already.

Achill. Thou art too brief, I will the fecond time
As I wou'd buy thee, view thee limb by limb.

  Hect. O, like a Book of fport thou read'ft me ore ;
But there's more in me then thou underftand'ft.

Achill. Tell me ye Heav'ns, in which part of his body
Shall I deftroy him ? there, or there, or there !
That I may give th' imagin'd wound a name,
And make diftinct the very breach, whereout

                          Hectors

Hettors great spirit flew ! answer me Heavens ! !

Hect. Wert thou an Oracle to tell me this !
I'de not believe thee, henceforth guard thee well,
I'le kill thee every where :
Ye Noble Grecians pardon me this boaft,
His infolence draws folly from my lips,
But I'le endeavour deeds to match thefe words ;
Elfe may I never.——

Ajax. Do not chafe thee Coufin,
And you *Achilles* let thefe threats alone :
You may have every day enough of Hettor,
If you have ftomack, the General State I fear
Can fcarce intreat you to perform your boaft.

Hect. I pray you let us fee you in the field ;
We have had paltry Wars, fince you refus'd
The Grecian caufe.

Achill. Doft thou entreat me Hettor !
To morrow will I meet thee fierce as death ;
To Night all peace.

Hect. Thy hand upon that match.

Agam. Firft all you Grecian Princes go with me,
And entertain great *Hettor*, afterwards,
As his own leafure, fhall concur with yours,
You may invite him to your feveral Tents.

           [*Exeunt* Agam. Hect. Menel. Neftor, Diomede, *together.*

Troil. My Lord *Ulyffes.*
Tell me I befeech you ;
In what part of the field does *Calchas* lodg !

Ulyff. At *Menelaus* Tent ;
There *Diomede* does feaft with him to Night :
Who neither looks on Heaven or on Earth,
But gives all gaze and bent of amorous view,
On *Creffida* alone.

Troil. Shall I, brave Lord be bound to you fo much
After we part from *Agamemnons* Tent.
To bring me thither !

Ulyff. I fhall wait on you.
As freely tell me, of what honour was
This *Creffida* in *Troy*? had fhe no Lovers there
Who mourn her abfence ?

Troil. O Sir, to fuch as boafting fhow their fcars,
Reproof is due, fhe lov'd and was belov'd :
That's all I muft impart. Lead on my Lord.

           [*Exeunt* Ulyffes Troilus.

Achill. to *Patro.* I'le heat his blood with Greckifh wine to Night,
                                                          Which

Which with my Sword I mean to cool to morrow.
Patroclus, let us feast him to the height.

Enter Thersites.

Patro. Here comes *Thersites.*

Achill. How now thou core of envy,
Thou crusty batch of Nature, what's the news?

Thers. Why thou picture of what thou seemst, thou Idoll of
Ideot worshippers, there's a Letter for thee.

Achill. From whence fragment?

Thers. Why thou full dish of fool, from *Troy.*

Patroc. Well said adversity! what makes thee so keen to day?

Thers. Because a fool's my whetstone.

Patro. Meaning me?

Thers. Yes meaning thy no meaning; prithee be silent, boy, I profit not by thy talk: Now the rotten diseases of the South, gut gripings,
ruptures, Catarrhs; loads of gravell in the back, Lethargies, cold
palsies, and the like, take thee, and take thee again ; thou green Sarce-
net flap for a sore eye, thou tassell of a prodigals purse, thou: Ah how
the poor world is pester'd with such water-flys: such diminitives of
nature.

Achill. My dear *Patroclus,* I am quite prevented
From my great purpose, bent on *Hector's* life :
Here is a Letter from my love *Polixena,*
Both taxing, and ingaging me to keep
An Oath that I have sworn : and will not break it
To save all Greece: let honour go or stay,
There's more Religion in my love than fame :

Exeunt Achilles, Patroclus.

Thers. With too much blood, and too little brain, these two are
running mad before the dog-days. There's *Agamemnon* too, an honest
fellow enough, and loves a brimmer heartily ; but he has not so much
brains as an old gander. But his brother *Menelaus,* there's a fellow :
the goodly transformation of *Iupiter* when he lov'd *Europa* : the primi-
tive Cuckold : A vile Monkey ty'd eternally to his brothers table. To
be a Dog, a Mule, a Cat, a toad, an Owle, a Lizard, a Herring without a roe, I wou'd not care : but to be *Menelaus* I wou'd conspire against
destiny——Hey day ! will with a wispe, and Jack a lanthorn !

Hector, Ajax, Agamemnon, Diomede, Ulisses, Troilus, *going with
torches over the stage.*

Agam. We go wrong ; we go wrong.

Ajax No, yonder 'tis ; there where we see the light.

Hect. I trouble you.

Ajax. Not at all Cousin : Here comes *Achilles* himself to guide us.

H

Enter

Enter Achilles.

Achill. Welcome brave *Hector*, welcome princes all :

Agam. So now, brave Prince of *Troy*, I take my leave ; *Ajax* commands the guard, to wait on you.

Men. Good night my Lord !

Hect. Good night Sweet Lord *Menelaus.*

Therf. afide. Sweet quoth a *!* fweet Sink, fweet fhore, fweet Jakes *!*

Achill. Neftor will ftay ; and you Lord *Diomede.* Keep *Hector* company an hour or two.

Diom. I cannot Sir *:* I have important bufinefs.

Achill. Enter my Lords.

Uliff. to Troil. Follow his torch : he goes to *Calchas's* tent.

[*Exeunt* Achill. Hect. Ajax *at one way,* Diomede, *another ; and after him* Ulyfs, Troylus.

Thers. This *Diomede's* a moft falfe-hearted rogue, an unjuft Knave : I will no more truft him when he winks with one eye, then I will a Serpent when he hiffes. He will fpend his mouth and pro- mife, like Brabbler the Hound : but when he performs, Aftronomers fet it down for a predigy ; Though I long to fee *Hector*, I cannot for- bear dogging him. They fay a keeps a *Trojan* Drabb : and ufes *Calchas* tent, that fugitive Prieft of *Troy* ; that Canonical Rogue of our fide. I'le after him : nothing but whoring in this Age : all incontinent Rafcalls *! Exit* Therfites.

Entere Calchas, Creffida.

Calch. O, what a blefling is a vertuous child *!* Thou haft reclam'd my mind, and calm'd my paffions Of anger and revenge : my love to *Troy* Revives within me, and my loft *Tyara* No more difturbs my mind :

Creff. A vertuous conqueft.

Calch. I have a womans longing to return But yet which way without your ayd I know not.

Creff. Time muft inftruct us how.

Calch. You muft diffemble love to *Diomede* ftill : Falfe *Diomede*, bred in *Ulyffes* School Can never be deceiv'd, But by ftrong Arts and blandifhments of love : Put 'em in practice all ; feem loft and won, And draw him on, and give him line again. This *Argus* then may clofe his hundred eyes And leave our flight more eafy.

Creff. How can I anfwer this to love and *Troilus ?*

Calch. Why 'tis for him you do it : promife largely ; That Ring he faw you wear, he much fufpects

Was

Was given you by a Lover; let him have it.

    Diom. within. Hoa; *Calchas, Calchas!*

    Calch. Hark! I hear his voice.

Purſue your project: doubt not the ſucceſs.

    Creſ. Heaven knows againſt my will: and yet my hopes

This night to meet my *Triolus*, while 'tis truce

Afford my minde ſome eaſe.

    Calch. No more: retire.   *Exit* Creſſida.

Enter Diomede; Troilus *and* Ulyſſes *appear liſtening at one door, and*
Therſites *watching at another.*

    Diom. I came to ſee your Daughter, worthy *Calchas.*

    Calch. My Lord I'le call her to you.   *Exit* Calchas.

    Ulyſſes to Troil. Stand where the torch may not diſcover us.

Enter Creſſida.

    Troil. Creſſida comes forth to him!

    Diom. How now my charge?

    Creſ. Now my ſweet Guardian: hark a word with you.

                             Whiſper.

    Troil. I, ſo familiar!

    Diom. Will you remember?

    Creſ. Remember: yes.

    Troil. Heav'ns! what ſhou'd ſhe remember! plague and madneſſe!

    Ulyſſes. Prince, you are mov'd: let us depart in time

Leſt your diſpleaſure ſhould enlarge it ſelf

To wrathfull terms: this place is dangerous;

The time unfit: 'beſeech you let us go.

    Troil. I pray you ſtay; by Hell, and by Hell torments

I will not ſpeak a word.

    Diom. I'le hear no more: good night.

    Creſ. Nay, but you part in anger!

    Troil. Does that grieve thee! O wither'd truth!

    Diom. Farewell Couſner.

    Creſ. Indeed I am not: pray come back again.

    Ulyſſ. You ſhake my Lord, at ſomething: will you go?

You will break out.

    Troil. By all the Gods I will not.

There is between my will and all my actions,

A guard of patience! ſtay a little while.

    Thers. aſide. How the devill luxury with his fat rump, and potato

finger, tickles theſe together! put him off a little, you fooliſh Harlot!

'twill ſharpen him the more.

    Diom. But will you then?

    Creſſi. I will as ſoon as ere the War's concluded.

Diom. Give me some token, for the surety of it :
The Ring I saw you wear.

   Cressi. Giving it. If you must have it.

   Troil. The Ring! nay then 'tis plain! O beauty where's thy faith *!*

   Ulyss. You have sworn patience.

   Thersi. That's well, that's well, the pledge is given, hold her to
her word good Devil, and her soul's thine I warrant thee.

   Diom. Who's waît ?

   Cressi. By all *Diana's* waiting train of stars,
And by her self, I will not tell you whose.

   Diom. Why then thou lov'st him still, farewell for ever :
Thou never shalt mock *Diomede* again.

   Cressi. You shall not go, one cannot speak a word
But straight it starts you.

   Diom. I do not like this fooling.

   Thersi. Nor I by *Pluto* : but that which likes not me, pleases me best.

   Diom. I shall expect your promise.

   Cressi. I'le perform it.
Not a word more, good night——I hope for ever :   [*aside.*
Thus to deceive deceivers is no fraud.

           [*Exeunt* Diomede Cressida *severally.*

   Ulyss. All's done my Lord.

   Troil. Is it ?

   Ulyss. Pray let us go.

   Troil. Was *Cressida* here ?

   Ulyss. I cannot conjure Trojan.

   Troil. She was not sure! she was not.
Let it not be believ'd for womanhood :
Think we had Mothers, do not give advantage,
To biting Satyr, apt without a theme,
For defamation, to square all the sex
By *Cressid's* rule, rather think this not *Cressida.*

   Thersi. Will he swagger himself out on's own eyes !

   Troil. This she ! no this was *Diomede's Cressida.*
If beauty have a Soul, this is not she :
I cannot speak for rage, that Ring was mine,
By Heaven I gave it, in that point of time
When both our joys were fullest !——if he keeps it
Let dogs eat *Troilus.*

   Thersi. He'll tickle it for his Concupy : this will be sport to see !
Patroclus will give me any thing for the intelligence of this whore ;
a parrot will not do more for an almond, than he will for a commodious drab : I would I cou'd meet with this Rogue *Diomede* too ; I wou'd
croke like a Raven to him ; I wou'd bode : it shall go hard but I'le
find him out.   *Exit* Thersites.

                                 Enter

Enter Æneas.

Æn. I have been seeking you this hour, my Lord :
Hector by this is arming him in *Troy.*

Ulyss. Commend me gallant *Troilus* to your Brother :
Tell him I hope he shall not need to arm :
The fair *Polixena* has by a letter
Disarm'd our great *Achilles* of his rage.

Troil. This I shall say to *Hector.*

Ulyss. So I hope !
Pray Heaven *Thersites* have inform'd me true,——— [*aside.*

Troil. Good night, my Lord ; accept distracted thanks.
[*Exit* Ulisses.

Enter Pandarus.

Pand. Hear ye, my Lord, hear ye ; I have been seeing yon poor girl.
There have been old doings there i'faith.

Troil. aside. Hold yet, my Spirits ; let him powr it in :
The poyson's kind : the more I drink of it
The sooner 'twill dispatch me.

Æne. to Pand. Peace you babbler !

Pand. She has been mightily made on by the *Greeks* : she takes most
wonderfully among 'em : *Achilles* kiss'd her, and *Patroclus* kiss'd her :
Nay and old *Nestor* put aside his gray beard and brush'd her with his
whiskers. Then comes me *Agamemnon* with his Generals Staff, diving
with a low bow e'en to the ground, and rising again, just at her lips :
And after him came *Ulysses*, and *Ajax*, and *Menelaus* : and they so
pelted her i'faith : pitter patter, pitter patter, as thick as hayl-stones.
And after that a whole rout of 'em : Never was woman in *Phrygia*
better kiss'd.

Troil. aside. *Hector* said true : I finde, I finde it now !

Pand. And last of all comes me *Diomede* so demurely : that's a notable sly Rogue I warrant him ! mercy upon us, how he layd her on upon the lips ! for as I told you, she's most mightily made on among the
Greekes. What, cheer up I say Man ! she has every ones good word. I
think in my conscience, she was born with a caull upon her head.

Troil. aside. Hell, death, confusion, how he tortures me !

Pand. And that Rogue-Priest my Brother, is so courted and treated for her sake : the young Sparks do so pull him about, and hall him
by the Cassock : nothing but invitations to his Tent, and his Tent,
and his Tent. Nay and one of 'em was so bold, as to ask him if she were
a Virgin, and with that the Rogue my Brother, takes me up a little
God in his hand, and kisses it ; and swears devoutly that she was, then
was I ready to burst my sides with laughing, to think what had pass'd
betwixt you two.

Troil. O I can bear no more : she's falshood all :
False by both kinds ; for with her mothers milk

She

She fuck'd th'infufion of her Fathers Soul.
She only wants an opportunity,
Her Soul's a whore already.

Pand. What wou'd you make a Monopoly of a womans lips: a little confolation or fo, might be allow'd one wou'd think in a lovers abfence!

Troil. Hence from my fight: let ignominy brand thy hated name:
Let Modeft Matrons at thy mention ftart;
And blufhing Virgins, when they read our Annals,
Skip o're the guilty page that holds thy Legend,
And blots the noble work.

Pand. O world, world; thou art an ungratefull patch of Earth!
Thus the poor Agent is defpis'd! he labours painfully in his calling,
and trudges between parties: but when their turns are ferv'd, come
out's too good for him. I am mighty melancholy: I'le e'en go home,
and fhut up my doors; and dye o'th fullens like an old bird in a Cage!
Exit Pandarus.

Enter Diomede *and* Therfites.

Thers. afide. There; there he is: now let it work: now play thy part
jealoufy, and twinge e'm: put 'em between thy milftones, and grinde
the Rogues together.

Diom. My Lord I am by *Ajax* fent to inform you
This hour muft end the truce.

Æneas to Troil. Contain your felf;
Think where we are.

Diom. Your ftay will be unfafe.

Troil It may for thofe I hate.

Therf. afide. Well faid *Trojan*: there's the firft hit.

Diom. Befeech you Sir make hafte, my own affairs
Call me another way.

Thers. afide. What affairs; what affairs; demand that, Dolthead! the
Rogue will lofe a quarrell for want of wit to ask that queftion.

Troil. May I enquire where your affairs conduct you?

Thers. afide. Well fayd again; I beg thy pardon.

Diom. Oh, it concerns you not.

Troil. Perhaps it does.

Diom. You are too inquifitive: nor am I bound
To fatisfy an Enemies requeft.

Troil. You have a Ring upon your finger *Diomede*,
And given you by a Lady,

Diom. If it were; 'Twas given to one who can defend her gift.

Thers. afide. So, fo; the boars begin to gruntle at one another: fet
up your briftles now a'both fides: whet and foam Rogues.

Troil. You muft reftore it *Greek*, by Heaven you muft:
No fpoil of mine fhall grace a Traitors hand.

And,

And, with it, give me back the broken vows
Of my falfe fair ; which, perjur'd as fhe is,
I never will refigne, but with my Soul.

    Diom. Then thou it feems art that forfaken fool
Who wanting merit to preferve her heart,
Repines in vain to fee it better plac'd ;
But know, (for now I take a pride to grieve thee)
Thou art fo loft a thing in her efteem
I never heard thee nam'd ; but fome fcorn follow'd :
Thou wert our table talk for laughing meals :
Thy name our fportful theme for Evening walks :
And intermiffive hours of cooler Love :
When hand in hand we went. [*Troil.*] Hell and furies !

    Therfi. Afide. O well ftung Scorpion !
Now *Menelaus* his Greek horns are out o' doors, there's a new Cuckold
ftart up on the Trojan fide.

    Troil. Yet this was fhe, ye Gods that very fhe,
Who in my arms lay melting all the Night ;
Who kifs'd and figh'd, and figh'd, and kifs'd again,
As if her Soul flew upward to her lips,
To meet mine there, and panted at the paffage.
Who loath to finde the breaking day, look'd out,
And fhrunk into my bofome, there to make
A little longer darknefs.

    Diom. Plagues and tortures !

    Therfi. Good, good, by *Pluto !* their fool's mad to lofe his harlot ;
and our fools mad, that tother fool had her firft : if I fought peace now,
I cou'd tell 'em there's punk enough to fatisfie 'em both : whore fuffici-
ent ! but let 'em worry one another, the foolifh currs ; they think they
can never have enough of carrion.

    Æneas. My Lords, this fury is not proper here,
In time of truce ; if either fide be injur'd
To morrow's Sun will rife apace, and then——

    Troil. And then ! but why fhould I defer till then ?
My blood calls now, there is no truce for Traytors.
My vengeance rowls within my breaft, it muft
It will have vent.——   [*Draws.*

    Diom Hinder us not *Æneas*,
My blood rides high as his, I truft thy honour ;
And know thou art too brave a foe to break it.——   [*Draws.*

    Therfi. Now Moon ! now fhine fweet Moon ! let 'em have juft light
enough to make their paffes : and not light enough to ward 'em.

    Æne. Drawing too. By Heav'n he comes on this who ftrikes the firft,
You both are mad, is this like gallant men
To fight at midnight ; at the Murderers hour ?

                                           When

When only guilt and rapine draws a Sword ?
Let night enjoy her dues of foft repofe ;
But let the Sun behold the brave mans courage.
And this I dare engage for *Diomede*
Foe though I am, he fhall not hide his head,
But meet you in the very face of danger.

    Diom. putting up. Be't fo: and were it on fome precipice
High as *Olympus*, and a Sea beneath
Call when thou dar'ft, juft on the fharpeft point
I'le meet, and tumble with thee to deftruction.

    Troil. A gnawing confcience haunts not guilty men
As I'le haunt thee, to fummon thee to this,
Nay, fhould'ft thou take the *Stygian lake* for refuge
I'le plunge in after, through the boiling flames
To pufh thee hiffing down the vaft Abyffe.

    Diom. Where fhall we meet ?

    Troil. Before the Tent of *Calchas* :
Thither, through all your Troops, I'le fight my way ;
And in the fight of perjur'd *Creffida*
Give death to her through thee.

    Diom. Tis largely promis'd.
But I difdain to anfwer with a boaft ;
Be fure thou fhalt be met.

    Troil. And thou be found.   [*Exeunt* Troilus, Æneas, *one way* :
                              Diomede *the other.*

    Thers. Now the furies take *Æneas*, for letting 'em fleep upon their quarrell : who knows but reft may cool their brains, and make 'em rife maukifh to mischief upon confideration ? May each of 'em dream he fees his Cockatrice in to'thers arms : and be ftabbing one another in their fleep, to remember 'em of their bufinefs when they wake : let 'em be punctual to the point of honour ; and if it were poffible let both be firft at the place of Execution. Let neither of 'em have cogitation e-nough, to confider 'tis a whore they fight for : and let 'em vallue their lives at as little as they are worth. And laftly let no fucceeding fools take warning by 'em ; but in imitation of them when a Strumpet is in queftion,

    Let 'em beneath thair feet all reafon trample ;
    And think it great to perifh by Example.   *Exit.*

A C T.

ACT V. SCENE I.

Hector, Trojans, Andromache.

Hect. THe blew mists rise from off the nether grounds,
And the Sun mounts apace : to arms, to arms :
I am resolv'd to put to th' utmost proof
The fate of *Troy* this day.

Andro. aside. Oh, wretched woman, oh!

Hect. Methought I heard you sigh, *Andromache* !

Andro. Did you my Lord ?

Hect. Did you my Lord ? you answer indirectly,
Just when I sayd that I wou'd put our fate
Upon th'extreamest proof, you fetch'd a groan ;
And, as you check'd your self, for what you did
You stifl'd it, and stopt. Come you are sad.

Andro. The Gods forbid.

Hect. What should the Gods forbid ?

Andro. That I shou'd give you cause of just offence.

Hect. You say well : but you look not cheerfully.
I mean this day to waste the stock of war,
And lay it prodigally out in blows :
Come gird my sword, and smile upon me, love ;
Like victory come flying to my arms ;
And give me earnest of desir'd successe.

Andro. The Gods protect you ; and restore you to me.

Hect. What, grown a Coward ! thou wert us'd, *Andromache,*
To give my courage, courage : thou woudst cry
Go *Hector* ; day grow's old ; and part of Fame
Is ravish'd from thee, by thy sloathfull stay.

Andro. aside. What shall I do, to seem the same I was !
Come let me gird thy fortune to thy side :
And conquest sit as close, and sure as this.

[*She goes to gird his Sword* ; *and it falls.*]

Now mercy, Heaven ! the Gods avert this omen !

Hect. A foolish omen ! take it up again ;
And mend thy errour.

Andro. I cannot : for my hand obeys me not.
But as in slumbers, when we fain wou'd run
From our imagin'd fears, our idle feet
Grow to the ground, our struggling voice dyes inward,
So now , when I wou'd force my self to cheat you
My faltring tongue can give no glad presage ;
Alas, I am no more *Andromache.*

I

Hect. **Why then thy former Soul is flown to me :**
For I, me thinks, am lifted into ayr :
As if my mind, maſtring my mortal part
Wou'd bear my exalted body to the Gods.
Laſt night I dreamt *Jove* ſate on *Ida's* top
And beckning with his hand divine from far,
He pointed to a quire of *Demi-*gods,
Bacchus, and *Hercules,* and all the reſt
Who free from humane toils had gain'd the pitch
Of bleſt eternity : lo there he ſayd ;
Lo there's a place for *Hector.*
   Andro. Be to thy Enemies this boding dream !
   Hect. Why it portends me honour and renoun.
   Andro. Such honour, as the Brave gain after death.
For I have dreamt all night of horrid ſlaughters,
Of trampling horſes, and of Charriot wheels
Wading in blood up to their Axeltrees.
Of fiery *Demons* gliding down the Skyes,
And *Ilium* brighten'd with a midnight blaze ;
O therefore, if thou lov'ſt me, go not forth.
   Hect. Go to thy bed again ; and there dream better.
Ho bid my Trumpet Sound.
   Andro. No notes of ſally for the Heaven's ſweet ſake.
Tis not for nothing when my Spirits droop :
This is a day when thy ill Starrs are ſtrong
When they have driv'n thy helpleſs genius down
The ſteep of Heaven to ſome obſcure retreat.
   Hect. No more ; ev'n as thou lov ſt my fame no more :
My honour ſtands ingag'd to meet *Achilles* :
What will the *Grecians* think ; or what will he,
Or what will *Troy* ; or what wilt thou thy ſelf
When once this ague fit of fear is ore ;
If I ſhould loſe my honour for a dream.
   Andro. Your Enemies too well your courage know,
And Heaven abhorrs the forfiet of raſh vows
Like ſpotted livers in a Sacrifice.
I cannot ; O I dare not let you go :
For when you leave me, my preſaging minde
Says, I ſhall never, never ſee you more.
   Hect. Thou excellently good, but oh too ſoft,
Let me not ſcape the danger of this day,
But I have ſtruggling in my manly Soul
To ſee thoſe modeſt tears, aſham'd to fall,
And witneſs any part of woman in thee !
And now I fear, leſt thou ſhould'ſt think it fear,

If thus diffwaded, I refufe to fight,
And ftay inglorious in thy arms at home.

Andro. Oh cou'd I have that thought I fhou'd not love thee;
Thy Soul is proof to all things but to kindnefs.
And therefore t'was that I forbore to tell thee
How mad *Caffandra*, full of prophecy
Ran round the ftreets, and like a Bacchanal
Cry'd hold him *Priam*, 'tis an ominous day,
Let him not go; for *Hector* is no more.

Hect. Our life is fhort but to extend that fpan
To vaft Eternity is virtues work.
Therefore to thee, aad not to fear of fate
Which once muft come to all, give I this day
But fee thou move no more the like requeft:
For reft affur'd that to regain this hour
To morrow will I tempt a double danger:
Mean time, let Deftiny attend thy leifure.
I reckon this one day a blank of of life.

Enter Troilus.

Troil. Where are you Brother? now in honour's name,
What do you mean to be thus long nnarm'd?
Th' imbattel'd Souldiers throug about the gates:
The Matrous to the turrets tops afcend
Holding their helpleffe children in their arms,
To make you early known to their young eyes,
And *Hector* is the univerfal fhout.

Hect. Bid all unarm, I will not fight to day.

Troil. Employ fome coward to bear back this news,
And let the children hoot him for his pains;
By all the gods and by my juft revenge,
This Sun fhall fhine the laft for them or us:
Thefe noify ftreets or yonder ecchoing plains
Shall be to morrow filent as the grave.

Andro. O Brother do not urge a brothers fate,
But let this rack of heav'n and earth rowl o're,
And when the ftorm is paft put out to fea.

Troil. Oh now I know from whence his change proceeds,
Some frantick Augur has obferv'd the skyes;
Some victim wants a heart, or crow flys wrong;
By heav'n 'twas never well fince fawcy Priefts
Grew to be Mafters of the liftning herd;
And into Miters cleft the Regal Crown.
Then as the Earth were fcanty for their pow'r,
They drew the pomp of Heav'n to wait on them;
Shall I go publifh *Hector* dares not fight

I 2

Becaufe

Becaufe a mad-man dreamt he talk'd with *Jove* ?
What cou'd the God fee in a brain-fick Prieft
That he fhould fooner talk to him then me?

Hect. You know my name's not liable to fear.

Troil. Yes, to the worft of fear, to fuperftition.
But whether thât or fondneffe of a wife,
(The more unpardonable ill) has feiz'd you,
Know this, the *Grecians* think you fear *Achilles*,
And that *Polixena* has beg'd your life.

Hect. How ! that my life is beg'd, and by my fifter ?

Troil. *Ulyffes* fo inform'd me at our parting,
With a malicious and difdainfull fmile :
'Tis true, he faid not in broad words you fear'd,
But in well-manner'd terms 'twas fo agreed
Achilles fhou'd avoid to meet with *Hector*.

Hect. He thinks my Sifters treafon, my petition,
That largely vaunting in my heat of bloud
More then I cou'd, it feems, or durft perform,
I fought evafion.

Troil. And in private pray'd.

Hect. O yes, *Polixena*, to beg my life.

Andro. He cannot think fo, do not urge him thus.

Hect. Not urge me! then thou think'ft I need his urging
By all the Gods fhou'd *Jove* himfelf defcend,
And tell me *Hector* thou deferv'ft not life
But take it as a boon ; I wou'd not live.
But that a Mortal man, and he of all men
Shou'd think my life were in his power to give,
I will not reft, till proftrate on the ground
I make him *Athieft*-like, implore his breath
Of me and not of Heaven.

Troil. Then you'l refufe no more to fight.

Hect. Refufe ! I'le not be hinder'd, Brother.
I'le through and through 'em, ev'n their hindmoft ranks.
Till I have found that large fiz'd boafting fool
Who dare prefume my life is in his gift.

Andro. Farewell, farewell : 'tis vain to ftrive with fate :
Caffandra's raging God infpires my breaft,
With truths that muft be told and not believ'd.
Look how he dyes ! look how his eye turns pale !
Look how his blood burfts out at many vents !
Hark how *Troy* roars, how *Hecuba* crys out
And widow'd I fill all the ftreets with fcreams !
Behold diftraction, frenzy and amazement,

Like

Like Antiques meet, and tumble upon heaps !
And all cry *Hector* ; *Hectors* dead ! Oh *Hector* !

[*Exit* Andromache.

Hect. What sport will be when we return at Evening,
To laugh her out of count'nance for her dreams !
  Troil. I have not quench'd my eyes with dewy sleep this Night ;
But fiery fumes mount upward to my brains,
And when I breathe, methinks my nostrills hiss !
I shall turn Basilisk ! and with my sight
Do my hands work, on *Diomede* this day.
  Hect. To Arms, to Arms, the vantguards are ingag'd :
Let us not leave one Man to guard the Walls,
Both Old and young, the coward and the brave,
Be Summond all, our utmost fate to try ;
And as one body move, whose Soul am I.

[*Exeunt.*

SCENE II. *The Camp.*

Alarm within.   *Enter* Agamemnon, Ulysses, Menelaus, Souldiers.

  Agam. THus far the promise of the day is fair :
       Æneas rather loses ground than gains,
I saw him overlabour'd, taking breath ;
And leaning on his spear, behold our Trenches
Like a fierce Lyon looking up to toyls,
Which yet he durst not leap.
  Ulyss. And therefore distant death does all the work :
The flights of whistling darts make brown the sky,
Whose clashing points strike fire, and guild the dusk :
Those that reach home, from neither host are vain,
So thick the prease ; so lusty are their arms,
That death seem'd never sent with better will !
Nor was with less concernment entertain'd.

Enter Nestor.

  Agam. Now *Nestor*, what's the news ?
  Nestor. I have descry'd,
A clow'd of dust that mounts in pillars upwards ;
Expanding as it travells to our Camp,
And from the midst I heard a bursting showt,
That rent the Heavens ! as if all *Troy* were swarm'd,
And on the wing this way.
  Menel. Let 'em come, let 'em come.
  Agam. Where's great *Achilles* !

Nest. .

Ulyss. Think not on *Achilles* :
Till *Hector* drag him from his Tent to fight,
(Which fure he will, for I have laid the train.)

Nest. But young *Patroclus* leads his Myrmydons ;
And in their front, ev'n in the face of *Hector,*
Refolves to dare the Trojans.

Agam. Hafte *Ulysses,* bid *Ajax* iffue forth, and fecond him.

Ulyss. Oh Noble General, let it not be fo.
Oppofe not rage, while rage is in its force ;
But give it way awhile ; and let it wafte :
The rifing deluge is not ftopt with dams,
Thofe it orebears, and drowns the hopes of harveft.
But wifely manag'd its divided ftrength
Is fluc'd in channels, and fecurely drain'd :
Firft, let fmall parties dally with their fury.
But when their force is fpent and unfupply'd
The refidue with mounds may be reftrain'd,
And dry-fhod, we may pafs the naked ford.

Enter Therfites.

Thers. Ho, ho, ho !

Menel. Why doft thou laugh, unfeafonable fool !

Thers. Why thou fool in feafon, cannot a man laugh, but thou thinkft
he makes horns at thee ! Thou Prince of the Herd, what haft thou to
do with laughing ! Tis the prerogative of man to laugh ! Thou Rifi-
bility without Reafon : thou fubject of laughter ; Thou fool Royall :

Ulys. But tell us the occafion of thy mirth?

Thers. Now a man asks me, I care not if I anfwer to my own kinde :
why the Enemies are broken into our Trenches : Fools like *Menelaus*
fall by thoufands ; yet not a humane Soul departs on either fide. *Troilus* and *Ajax* have almoft beaten one anothers heads off ; but are both
immortal for want of brains. *Patroclus* has kill'd *Sarpedon* ; and *Hector
Patroclus* : So there's a towardly fpringing fop gone off : He might
have made a Prince one day : But now he's nipt in the very budd and
promife of a moft prodigious Coxcomb.

Agam. Bear off *Patroclus* body to *Achilles* :
Revenge will arm him now, and bring us ayd.
Th'alarm Sounds near ; and fhouts are driv'n upon us,
As of a crowd confus'd in their retreat.

Ulys. Open your Ranks, and make thefe mad men way :
Then clofe again, to charge upon their backs :
And quite confume the Reliques of the warr.

[*Exeunt all but* Therfites.

Thers. What fhoales of fools one battle fweeps away !
How it purges families of younger Brothers ! Highways of Robbers,
and

and Cities of Cuckold-makers ! There's nothing like a pitch'd Battle, for these brisk Addle-heads ! Your Physitian is a pretty fellow ; but his fees make him tedious ; he rids not fast enough ; the fools grow upon him, and their horse bodies are poyson proof. Your Pestilence is a quicker Remedy ; but it has not the grace to make distinction ; it huddles up honest men and Rogues together. But your battle has dis-cretion ; it picks out all the forward fools. And sowses 'em together into Immortality.

[Shouts and alarm within.

Plague upon these drums and Trumpets ! these sharp sawces of the War, to get fools an Appetite to fighting ! what do I among 'em ? I shall be mistaken for some valiant Asse , and dye a Martyr, in a wrong Religion !

Here Grecians fly over the stage, pursued by Trojans : One
Trojan turns back upon Thersites who is flying too.

Trojan. Turn slave and fight.

Thers. turning. What art thou !

Troj. A Bastard Son of Priam's.

Thers. I am a Bastard too : I love Bastards : I am Bastard in body, Bastard in minde, Bastard in valour ; in every thing illegitimate. A Bear will not fasten upon a Bear ; why should one Bastard offend a-nother ! let us part fair, like true Sons of Whores ; and have the fear of our Mothers before our eyes.

Troj. The Devil take thee Coward.　　　　　　　　　Exit Trojan

Thers. Now wou'd I were either Invisible, or invulnerable ? these Gods have a fine time on't ; they can see and make mischief, and ne-ver feel it.

[Clattring of swords at both doors ; he runs each way,
and meets the noise.

A pox clatter you ; I am compass'd in ! Now wou'd I were that block-head <i>Ajax</i> for a minute : some sturdy <i>Trojan</i> will poach me up with a long pole ! and then the Rogues may kill one another upon free cost, and have no body left to laugh at 'em :
Now Destruction ! now Destruction !

Enter Hector and Troilus driving in the Greeks .

Hect. to Ther. Speak what part thou fightst on !

Thers. I fight not at all : I am for neither side.

Hect. Thou art a Greek : art thou a match for Hector. Art thou of blood and honour ?

Thers. No, I am a rascall : a scurvy railing knave ; a very filthy Rogue.

Hect. I do believe thee ; live.

Thers. God a mercy, that thou wilt believe me : but the Devil break thy neck for frighting me :　　　　　　[aside.

Troilus

Troilus returning. What Prifoner have you there?

Hect. A gleaning of the war : a Rogue he fays.

Troil. Difpatch him and away. [*going to kill him.*

Thers. Hold, hold : what is't no more but difpatch a man and away! I am in no fuch haft : I will not dye for *Greece* ; I hate *Greece,* and by my good will wou'd nere have been born there ; I was miftaken into that Country, and betray'd by my parents to be born there. And befides I have a mortal Enemy amongft the *Grecians,* one *Diomede* a damned villain, and cannot dye with a fafe confcience till I have firft murther'd him.

Troil. Shew me thrt *Diomede* and thou fhalt live.

Therf. Come along with me and I'le conduct thee to *Calchas* his Tent , where I believe he's now making warre with the Priefts daughter.

Hect. Here we muft part, our deftinies divide us ;
Brother and friend, farewell.

Troil. When fhall we meet?

Hect. When the Gods pleafe: if not, we once muft part.
Look ; on yon hill their fquander'd Troops unite ;

Troil. If I miftake not, 'tis their laft Referve :
The ftorm's blown ore ; and thofe but after drops.

Hect. I wifh our Men be not too far ingag'd :
For few we are and fpent ; as having born
The burden of the Day : but hap what can
They fhall be charg'd : *Achilles* muft be there ;
And him I feek, or death.
Divide our Troops ; and take the frefher half.

Troil. O Brother,

Hect. No difpute of Ceremony !
Thefe are enow for me ; in faith enow :
There bodies fhall not flag while I can lead ;
Nor wearied limbs confefs mortality,
Before thofe Ants that blacken all yon hill
Are crept into their Earth : Farewell. *Exit Hector.*

Troil. Farewell ; come Greek :

Therf. Now thefe Rival-rogues will clapperclaw one another, and I fhall have the fport on't. *Exit* Troil. *with* Therfites.

Enter Achilles *and* Myrmidons.

Achil. Which way went *Hector* ?

Myrmyd. Up yon fandy hill :
You may difcern 'em by their fmoaking track ;
A wavering body working with bent hams
Againft the rifing, fpent with painfull march,
And by loofe-footing caft on heaps together.

Achil.

Achill. O thou art gone! thou sweetest, best of friends;
Why did I let thee tempt the shock of war
Ere yet thy tender nerves had strung thy limbs,
And knotted into strength. Yet, though too late,
I will, I will revenge the, my *Patroclus*!
Nor shall thy Ghost thy Murtherer's long attend,
But thou shalt hear him calling *Charon* back,
Ere thou art wafted to the farther shore.
Make hast, my Soldiers: give me this days pains.
For my dead friend: strike every hand with mine,
Till *Hector* breathless, on the ground we lay!
Revenge is honour, the securest way.　　　*Exit with* **Myrmidons.**

[*Enter* Thersites, Troilus, Trojans.

Thers. That's *Calcha's* tent.
Troil. Then that one spot of Earth contains more falshood
Than all the Sun sees in his race beside.
That I shou'd trust the Daughter of a Priest!
Priesthood, that makes a Merchandise of Heaven!
Priesthood that sells eve'n to their prayr's and blessings!
And forces us to pay for our own cousnage!
Thers. Nay cheats Heav'n too with entrails and with offals;
Gives it the garbidge of a Sacrifice
And keeps the best for private Luxury.
Troil. Thou hast deserv'd thy life, for cursing Priests:
Let me embrace thee; thou art beautifull:
That back, that nose; those eyes are beautiful:
Live, thou art honest; for thou hat'st a Priest.
Thers. aside. Farewell Trojan; if I scape with life, as I hope; **and**
thou art knock'd o'th head, as I hope too; I shall be the first that **ever**
scap'd the revenge of a Priest, after cursing him; and thou wilt not **be**
the last, I Prophecy that a Priest will bring to ruin.　　[*Exit* Ther.
Troil. Me thinks my soul is rowz'd to her last work:
Has much to do, and little time to spare.
She starts within me, like a Traveller
Who sluggishly out-slept his morning hour
And mends his pace, to reach his Inn betimes.

Noise within, follow, follow.

A Noise of Arms! the Traitor may be there:
Or else, perhaps, that conscious scene of Love,
The Tent may hold him, yet I dare not search
For oh I fear to find him in that place.　　　[*Exit.* Troilus.

Enter Calchas, Cressida.

Cress. Where is he? I'le be justify'd or dye.

K

Calch.

Calch. So quickly vanish'd ! he was here but now :
He muſt be gone to ſearch for *Diomede*,
For *Diomede* told me, here they were to fight.
   Creſſ. Alas ! (*Calch.*) you muſt prevent, and not complain.
   Creſſ. If *Troilus* dye, I have no ſhare in life.
   Calch. If *Diomede* ſink beneath the ſword of *Troilus*,
We loſe not only a Protector here,
But are debard all future means of flight.
   Creſſi. What then remains !
   Calch. To interpoſe betimes
Betwixt their ſwords; or if that cannot be
To intercede for him, who ſhall be vanquiſh'd,
Fate leaves no middle courſe.——   *Exit.* Calchas.

Claſhing within.

   Creſſi. Ah me I hear e'm ;
And fear 'tis paſt prevention.
   Enter Diomede, *retiring before* Troilus, *and falling as he enters.*
   Troil. Now beg thy life, or dye.
   Diom. No : uſe thy fortune :
I loath the life, which thou canſt give, or take.
   Troil. Scornſt thou my mercy villain !——take thy wiſh.——
   Creſſi. Hold, hold your hand my Lord, and hear me ſpeak.

   Troilus *turns back : in which time* Diomede *riſes : Trojans and Greeks enter, and rank themſelves on both ſides of their Captains.*

   Troil. Did I not hear the voice of perjur'd *Creſſida* ?
Com'ſt thou to give the laſt ſtab to my heart ?
As if the proofs of all thy former falſhood
Were not enough convincing, com'ſt thou now
To beg my Rivals life !
Whom, oh, if any ſpark of truth remain'd,
Thou coud'ſt not thus, ev'n to my face prefer !
   Creſſi. What ſhall I ſay ! that you ſuſpect me falſe
Has ſtruck me dumb ! but let him live my *Troilus*,
By all our loves, by all our paſt endearments
I do adjure thee ſpare him.
   Troil. Hell, and death !
   Creſſi. If ever I had pow'r to bend your mind,
Believe me ſtill your faithful *Creſſida* :
And though my innocence appear like guilt,
Becauſe I make his forfeit life my ſuit,
'Tis but for this, that my return to you
Wou'd be cut off for ever by his death.
My father, treated like a ſlave and ſcorn'd,

My

My self in hated bonds a Captive held.

Troil. Cou'd I believe thee, cou'd I think thee true
In triumph wou'd I bear thee back to *Troy*,
Though *Greece* could rally all her shatter'd troops,
And stand embatteld to oppose my way.
But, Oh, thou Syren, I will stop my ears
To thy enchanting notes; the winds shall bear
Upon their wings, thy words more light then they.

Cressi. Alass I but dissembled love to him;
If ever he had any proof beyond
What modesty might give.——

Diom. No! witnesse this——— (*the Ring shown.*)
There, take her Trojan; thou deserv'st her best,
You good, kind-natur'd, well-believing fools
Are treasures to a woman.
I was a jealous, hard vexatious Lover
And doubted ev'n this pledge till full possession:
But she was honourable to her word;
And I have no just reason to complain.

Cressi. O, unexampled, frontlesse impudence!

Troil. Hell show me such another tortur'd wretch, as *Troilus!*

Diom. Nay, grieve not: I resigne her freely up:
I'm satisfi'd: and dare engage for *Cressida*,
That if you have a promise of her person,
She shall be willing to come out of debt.

Cressi. [*kneeling.*] My only Lord: by all those holy vows
Which if there be a pow'r above are binding,
Or, if there be a Hell below, are fearful,
May every imprecation, which your rage
Can wish on me, take place, if I am false.

Diom. Nay, since you're so concern'd to be believ'd,
I'm sorry I have press'd my charge so far;
Be what you wou'd be thought: I can be grateful.

Troil. Grateful! Oh torment! now hells blewest flames
Receive her quick; with all her crimes upon her.
Let her sink spotted down. Let the dark host
Make room; and point: and hisse her, as she goes.
Let the most branded Ghosts of all her Sex
Rejoyce, and cry, here comes a blacker fiend.
Let her——

Cressi. Enough my Lord; you've said enough:
This faithlesse, perjur'd, hated *Cressida*,
Shall be no more, the subject of your Curses:
Some few hours hence, and grief had done your work;
But then your eyes had miss'd the satisfaction

Which

Which thus I give you——thus—— [*She ſtabs her ſelf they both run to her.*
  Diom. Help ; ſave her, help.
  Creſſi. Stand off ; and touch me not, thou Traitor, *Diomede :*
But you, my only *Troilus* come near :
Truſt me the wound which I have giv'n this breaſt
Is far leſſe painful, then the wound you gave it.
Oh, can you yet believe, that I am true !
  Troil. This were too much, ev'n if thou hadſt been falſe !
But, Oh, thou pureſt, whiteſt innocence,
(For ſuch I know thee now) too late I know it !
May all my curſes, and ten thouſand more
Heavier than they, fall back upon my head,
Pelion and *Oſſa* from the Gyants graves,
Be torn by ſome avenging Deity,
And hurld at me, a bolder wretch then they,
Who durſt invade the Skys !
  Creſſi. Hear him not Heavens !
But hear me bleſs him with my lateſt breath ;
And ſince I queſtion not your hard decree,
That doom'd my days unfortunate and few,
Add all to him, you take away from me ;
And I dye happy that he thinks me true.   [*Dyes.*
  Troil. She's gone for ever, and ſhe bleſt me dying !
Cou'd ſhe have curs'd me worſe ! ſhe dy'd for me ;
And like a woman, I lament for her :
Diſtraction pulls me ſeveral ways at once,
Here pity calls me to weep out my eyes ;
Deſpair then turns me back upon my ſelf,
And bids me ſeek no more, but finiſh here :   [*Sword to his breaſt.*
Ha, ſmilſt thou Traitor, thou inſtruct'ſt me beſt,
And turn'ſt my juſt revenge to puniſh thee.
  Diom. Thy worſt, for mine has been before hand with thee,
I triumph in thy vain credulity,
Which levels thy deſpairing ſtate to mine :
But yet thy folly to believe a foe ;
Makes thine the ſharper, and more ſhamefull loſs.
  Troil. By my few moments of remaining life ;
I did not hope for any future joy,
But thou haſt given me pleaſure ere I dye :
To puniſh ſuch a Villain.——Fight a part.   [*To his Souldiers.*
For Heaven and hell have mark'd him out for me,
And I ſhou'd grudg ev'n his leaſt drop of blood,
To any other hand.——

[Troilus *and* Diomede *fight, and both parties engage at the same time : The Trojans make the Greeks retire, and* Troilus *makes* Diomede *give ground and hurts him,* Trumpets *found,* Achilles *Enters with his Myrmidons, on the backs of the Trojans, who fight in a Ring encompaſs'd round :* Troilus *ſingling* Diomede *gets him down and kills him : and* Achilles *kills* Troilus *upon him. All the Trojans dye upon the place,* Troilus *laſt.*

Enter Agamemnon, Menelaus, Uliſſes, Neſtor, Ajax, *and Attendants.*

Achill. Our toyls are done, and thoſe aſpiring Walls
(The work of Gods, and almoſt mateing Heaven,)
Muſt crumble into rubbiſh on the plain.
Agam. When mighty *Hector* fell beneath thy Sword,
Their Old foundations ſhook, their nodding Towers
Threatned from high, the amaz'd Inhabitants :
And Guardian Gods for fear forſook their fanes.
Achill. Patroclus, now be quiet : *Hectors* dead :
And as a ſecond offring to thy Ghoſt,
Lyes *Troilus* high upon a heap of ſlain :
And noble *Diomede* beneath ; whoſe death
This hand of mine reveng'd.
Ajax. Reveng'd it baſely.
For *Troilus* fell by multitudes oppreſt ;
And ſo fell *Hector*, but 'tis vain to talk.
Ulyſſ. Hayl *Agamemnon !* truly Victor now !
While ſecret envy, and while open pride,
Among thy factious Nobles diſcord threw ;
While publique good was urg'd for private ends,
And thoſe thought Patriots, who diſturb'd it moſt ;
Then like the headſtrong horſes of the Sun,
That light which ſhou'd have cheer'd the World, conſum'd it :
Now peacefull order has reſum'd the reynes,
Old time looks young, and Nature ſeems renew'd :
     Then, ſince from homebred Factions ruine ſprings,
     Let Subjects learn obedience to their Kings.
                                   [*Exeunt Omnes.*

The

The Epilogue.

Spoken by Thersites.

THese cruel Critiques put me into passion;
  For in their lowring looks I reade damnation :
Ye expect a Satyr, and I seldom fail,
When I'm first beaten, 'tis my part to rail.
You British fools, of the Old Trojan stock,
That stand so thick one cannot miss the flock,
Poets have cause to dread a keeping Pit,
When Womens Cullyes come to judge of Wit.
As we strow Rats-bane when we vermine fear,
'Twere worth our cost to scatter fool-bane here.
And after all our judging Fops were serv'd,
Dull Poets too shou'd have a dose reserv'd,
Such Reprobates, as past all sence of shaming
Write on, and nere are satisfy'd with damming,
Next, those, to whom the Stage does not belong
Such whose Vocation onely is to Song ;
At most to Prologue, when for want of time
Poets take in for Journywork in Rhime.
But I want curses for those mighty shoales,
Of scribling Chlorisses, and Phillis fools,
Those Ophs shou'd be restraind, during their lives,
From Pen and Ink, as Madmen are from knives :
I cou'd rayl on, but 'twere a task as vain
As Preaching truth at Rome, or wit in Spain,
Yet to huff out our Play was worth my trying,
John Lilbourn scap'd his Judges by defying :
If guilty, yet I'm sure oth' Churches blessing,
By suffering for the Plot, without confessing.

FINIS.

Books Lately Printed.

COntemplations upon the remarkable Paſſages in the New Teſtament, Conſiſting in Divine Meditations up- on the Life of the Holy Jeſus. Writen by the Biſhop of *Exeter*.

Ten Tragical Hiſtories, Containing *Gods Revenge againſt the sin of Adultery*, Illuſtrated with Cuts.

Plays.

The Feign'd Curtezans, *Or,* A Nights Intrigue.

Sir Patient Fancy.

The Counterfeits.

Brutus of *Alba*, a Tragedy, By M.*Tate*. Acted at the Dukes Theatre.

All theſe Printed for *Jacob Tonſon* at the *Judges Head* at *Chancery-Lane End* next *Fleetſtreet*.

Medulla Hiſtoriæ Anglicanæ, Being a comprehenſive Hi- ſtory of the Lives and Reigns of the Monarchs of *England*, from the time of the Conqueſt thereof by *Julius Cæſar* to this preſent Year, 1679. With an Abſtract of the Lives of the Roman Emperors Commanding in *Britain*. To which is added, A Liſt of the Names of the Preſent Members of Parliament. Printed for *Abel Swall* at the *Unicorn* at the Weſt-End of S. *Pauls*.